Rhys Carpenter

PENGUIN BOOKS

Penguin Books Ltd, Harmondsworth,
Middlesex, England
Penguin Books Inc., 7110 Ambassador Road,
Baltimore, Maryland 21207, U.S.A.
Penguin Books Australia Ltd, Ringwood,
Victoria, Australia

First published 1970
Copyright © Rhys Carpenter, 1970

Designed by Gerald Cinamon
Printed in the United States of America by
Universal Lithographers Inc.
Set in Monotype Garamond

PELICAN BOOKS

THE ARCHITECT AND SOCIETY
Edited by John Fleming and Hugh Honour

The Architects of the Parthenon

Rhys Carpenter, M.A. (Oxon), Ph.D., Litt.D., was born in Massachusetts in 1889, and was educated at Columbia University and Balliol College, Oxford. He has been professor at a number of universities and schools both in the States and in Europe: Bryn Mawr College, Pennsylvania (1918–55), Classical School, American Academy, Rome (1926–7, 1939–40), University of California (1944–5), University of Pennsylvania (1960), University of Pittsburgh (1961–2), and the University of Washington (1963–4). He was attached to the American Commission to negotiate peace at Paris from 1918 to 1919, as an expert on Greco–Albanian territorial problems. He was also Director of the American School for Classical Studies at Athens (1927–32, 1946–8). In 1969 he became gold medallist of the Archaeological Institute of America. He is a member of such societies as the Hispanic Society of America, the Pontifical Roman Academy of Archaeology, the German Archaeological Society, and the American Philosophical Society. Professor Carpenter's most recent publications have been: *Greek Art: A Study in the Evolution of Style* (1963), *Discontinuity in Greek Civilization* (1966), and *Beyond the Pillars of Heracles* (1966). His numerous articles on Greek art have appeared in the *American Journal of Archaeology* and elsewhere. In his spare time, he enjoys mountain-climbing and archaeological exploration.

The Architects of the Parthenon

To Lucy Shoe Meritt and Benjamin Dean Meritt
for sharing their unrivalled knowledge of their respective specialties

Contents

Acknowledgements

For permission to use the illustrations in this volume acknowledgement is made to the following: James Austin, 45; Bildarchiv Foto Marburg, 7, 8, 52, 71; British Museum, 19, 20, 21, 22, 23, 28, 30, 31, 62, 70; Camera Press Ltd (photograph by Bernard G. Silberstein) 2, and back cover; Rhys Carpenter, 72; J. Allen Cash, 12; Deutsches Archaeologisches Institut, Rome, 48; École Française d'Archéologie, Athens, 42; Alison Frantz, 18, 29, 41, 44, 51, 56, 57, 64; John R. Freeman & Co., 58–61; Hirmer Fotoarchiv, Munich, 50, 53, 63, 67, 68; Mansell Collection, 6; Staatliches Museum, Berlin, 34, 35; Edwin Smith, 11, 25, 36, 37; E. M. Stresow-Czakó, 1, 13, 26, 27, 47, 49; John Webb, 24.

For Kallikrates the author acknowledges his debt to Ione M. Shear's penetrating article in Hesperia, xxxii (1963).

The plans and engravings have been reproduced with the permission of the following: Harvard University Press for diagrams 14, 15 and 33 taken from Lucy T. Shoe, *Profiles of Greek Mouldings*; Hirmer Verlag München for diagrams 17, 55, 66, and 69 taken from Berve–Gruben, *Greek Temples, Theatres, and Shrines*; the following plans have been redrawn by Paul White, 3, 4, 5, 32, 38, 39, 75.

The passages from *Greek Art* by Rhys Carpenter quoted in Note 7 are reproduced by permission of the University Press, University of Pennsylvania.

Title page engraving of a Doric capital and fragment of metope from the Parthenon is taken from Stuart and Revett, *Antiquities of Athens* (1762).

Illustrations

Foreword

A new book about the Parthenon might hardly be expected to offer anything very novel about a monument that has been subjected so often and so minutely to the scrutiny of scholars and laymen alike. And yet it can be shown that much has been overlooked and much has been wrongly interpreted in this symbol of the Greek genius, which has come to be accepted as the very epitome of Greek architectural art. Actually, its own incomparable renown through post-Renaissance centuries into modern times and its widespread acceptance as a typical example of the classic Greek ideal of embodying an architectural theme in intellectualized logical form have made it extremely difficult to look at its still beautiful ruin without preconceived ideas – unless, as in the present work, we take the trouble of first studying its intricate constructional history with its disillusioning political involvement and examine without prejudice the details of its deceptively simple Doric Order. If we are prepared to do this, we shall discover that many generally accepted notions about the Parthenon will have to be modified or altogether abandoned. For the historical reality is very different from the traditional view.

In particular, we must divest ourselves of all classicistic theories such as those evolved by the Renaissance and operative until quite recent times, even though some of these may pretend to derive from the Parthenon itself. We must bear in mind that while the Parthenon is a product of imaginative thinking, its idealism is not that of the Renaissance humanists, since its logical relations are concretely visual rather than abstractly mathematical. Although its proportions are eminently harmonious, they are not so in the manner advocated in the sixteenth century by Palladio, who followed the system of fixed arithmetical ratios propounded by Vitruvius in Augustan Rome and borrowed by him from late-Greek theorizing architects such as Hermogenes. In contrast to such stultifying adherence to exactly measurable ratios, the builders of the Parthenon worked empirically, trimming and fitting together the component marble blocks of the exterior and interior Orders, of the tapering walls and coffered ceilings, quite as much by eye and by immediate need as by previous theoretic calculation. The common belief that the Parthenon embodies a bewilderingly complex schedule of minutely exact measurements without deviation or error is entirely false. As common sense might have told us, Athena's resplendently coloured marble dwelling-place was built for the human eye to behold, not for the calculating brain or the divine intelligence to contemplate.

We need only examine the carefully controlled measurements recorded for the Parthenon by professional students of architecture to convince ourselves that the spacing of the exterior columns is irregular and that there is no consistent precision in the width of the metopes and cornice blocks. This immediately raises the question whether these deviations from the calculable average norm were the result of indifference and careless workmanship or, on the contrary, were the product of some unrecoverable mathematical scheme of variable ratios. The present study reaches the conclusion that neither of these alternatives supplies the correct answer. The departure from strict uniformity was entirely intentional: in view of the exquisite precision with which the profiles of the crowning mouldings were carved and the capitals of the columns were cut to geometrically true conic sections, and the column shafts and the tapering wall surfaces were made to lean, and – most delicate of all – a barely discernible convexity was added to the outline of the diminishing columns, it would be preposterous to accuse the architect of carelessness in spacing his columns or in controlling the dimensions of the individual blocks with which he put together his Order. And yet, while the deviations from exact uniformity must have been intentional, at the same time they were deliberately casual and designedly unsystematic, having been taken at random for a purely aesthetic purpose, in order to temper lifeless mathematical rigidity with those minute irregularities which distinguish the living organism from its abstract generic pattern – even as every leaf on an oak tree or a maple or any other arboreal species displays the same generic structural pattern, yet amid all its many thousand leaves no two are absolutely identical. The patternization of the Greek Doric Order is so severely simple and so repetitious that it would be sensed as emotionally cold and lifeless unless something were added to give it an effect of pulsating vitality.

Two related aesthetic devices were introduced for imparting a feeling of elasticity to the formally rigid lines of the Doric Order. These were firstly the barely perceptible convexity of entasis applied to the profile of the diminishing column shafts and secondly, even less appreciable, the light horizontal upward curvature to which the steps on the temple platform and the entablature above the columns were aligned.

It is in these subtle yet remarkably effective inventions for vitalizing a constructional system which is so severely simple that it verges on monotony, and in the superb, sculpturally inspired, treatment of its once shimmering white marble, that the Parthenon stands out above all other Doric temples of antiquity. For in other respects it cannot lay claim to any originality of personal invention or artistic imagination. There is little or nothing in the Parthenon (except the unrivalled sculptural adornment of its pediments and its wallcrown frieze) that cannot be matched in other Doric temples of the period. For it is a peculiar characteristic of Greek architecture that, in comparison with the differences apparent in any two Gothic cathedrals constructed within the same few decades, two Greek Doric temples are virtually indistinguishable one from another. The so-called temple of Poseidon at Paestum in southern Italy is so closely identical with the temple of Zeus at Olympia in mainland Greece, as restored graphically, that except for a slight discrepancy in absolute size only the specialist in Greek architecture can point to any difference. Nor does the Parthenon depart from this same canonic form except for the inclusion of a second chamber behind the main sanctuary room. In erecting it, Iktinos made no attempt at original disposition of interior space or unusual exterior appearance. His aim was not to produce a novel form for a temple but by utmost care and attention to detail to perfect the already established one.

The really unique and hitherto unsuspected feature of the Parthenon which I now put forward in this book is the discovery that it was a rebuilding, on enlarged scale, of an already partially completed temple by a different architect. There were *two* architects for the Parthenon because there were *two* Parthenons, with the later building incorporating the earlier one by re-using much of its material.

In consequence a considerable element of empirical improvisation entered into the creation of this building which, on uninformed inspection of its makeshift anomalies, has been thought to depend on the most carefully calculated mathematical relationships and the most delicately and minutely adjusted proportions. So far is this from being the case, that, as we shall see, the architect incorporated metopes from a previous building and even re-used columns designed and intended for a differently planned and differently proportioned temple.

This book is an attempt to discover the true history of the Parthenon and to show that fortune (or misfortune) made it a battleground for the two inimically opposed political factions of fifth-century Athens controlled by two historically great leaders – one an illustrious warrior, Kimon, the other an astute and unscrupulous politician, Pericles. It is for the reader to decide for himself how far the documented findings of this rather intricate investigation alter his conception not only of the Parthenon itself but of the potentialities of the Doric style and the aesthetic character of Greek architectural art.

The Architects of the Parthenon

1 (overleaf). Acropolis, general view from the north-west

1: The Parthenon of Kallikrates

For more than a hundred miles the modern motor road from Patras to Athens runs beside the sea until, after Eleusis, it finally turns away to ascend the pine-clad ridge of Mt Aigaleos. From the top, beyond. the little Byzantine church of Daphni, there suddenly opens a view across the Attic plain with Athens in the middle ground and Mt Hymettos against the horizon sky. After nightfall a million electric lights will make magic of the scene. But during day-time closer approach will bring disenchantment at sight of the welter of houses without architectural distinction lining crowded narrow streets. Yet disillusion at sight of the modern city gives place, even before the city is entered, to a breath-taking glimpse above the red-tiled roofs where, high on its bare outcropping of rock, clear and brilliant in the sunlight gleams the columned Parthenon [2].

2. Acropolis, general view from the Hill of the Muses

One may climb the Acropolis many times and examine its famous triad of fifth-century architectural masterpieces – Propylaea, Erechtheion, and Parthenon – without ever suspecting that the first far-away impression that Athena's temple perches on the exact summit of the Acropolis rock is not literally true, since actually it is raised aloft on a huge foundation of invisible masonry [3].

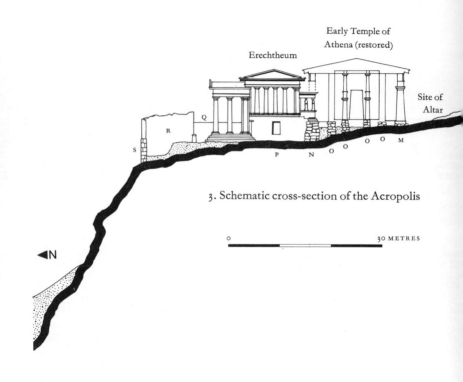

3. Schematic cross-section of the Acropolis

This great substructure, covering an area roughly 250 feet long and 100 feet wide (82 metres long and 30·5 metres wide) and in part built up to a height of more than 30 feet (9·75 metres) over bed rock, now lies (except for its topmost courses) wholly hidden underground, much as it was throughout Antiquity after the Parthenon was raised upon it. But, rather recently, the long southern flank of its great pile of squared

Parthenon

A. Stoa in front of the sacred cave
    and spring of Asklepios
B. Cave with the sacred spring
C. Wall of Kimon
D. Primitive polygonal wall
E. Fifth-century retaining wall
F. Primitive stratum of earth
G, H. Made earth of the fifth century
J. Podium of the older Parthenon
K. Chief cella of the Parthenon
L. Rock-cut rain-water cistern
M, N. Peristyle of the early temple of Athena
N. North peristyle wall, on which the caryatid porch rests
O. Original cella walls of the early temple
P. Pandroseion, at the west of the Erechtheum
Q. Flight of 12 steps to the higher level at the east
R. Acropolis wall rebuilt in modern times
S. Part of the Acropolis built by Pericles
    with very long blocks of porous stone

limestone blocks stood exposed, laid bare by modern probing into the unexpectedly deep adjoining soil.

More than a century ago – to be specific, in 1835–6, 1845, and again in 1859–60 and 1864 – exploratory pits and trenches were dug along the southern flank of the Parthenon; but it was not until 1885–90 that systematic excavation of the entire surface of the Acropolis adequately exposed the great masonry platform, revealing the existence of a series of walls deep underground, running roughly parallel to the platform at varying distances from it. It can be shown (*see* Note 1 on page 160) that these underground walls, some of which were fortification walls and some mere retaining walls, were erected in the order indicated by the Arabic numerals attached to them in diagram [4] – namely 1. Mycenaean, 2. polygonal, 3. ashlar, 4. Kimonian, and 5. Periclean. However, this chronological sequence will not be of much help unless some actual dates can be established for their construction. And it may not be immediately evident how this can be done, since (except for the varying styles of their masonry) the walls are in themselves timeless.

Yet some insight into their chronology might conceivably be gained by examining the mass of miscellaneous material thrown in behind them for terracing the steep fall between the high temple platform and the fortification wall of the Acropolis. For there was unearthed, imbedded under the modern surface here, a great variety of discarded material – chips from the dressing of marble and limestone building blocks, broken pieces of statuary and terracotta, and (most significant of all) enormous quantities of broken pottery carrying well-preserved painted ornaments and pictorial designs. If the date of production of this pottery could be fixed, this would yield at least an approximate estimate of the time when the fill was made.

Unfortunately, at the period when the area was excavated, although quite extensive records of the contents were kept as the work progressed, there was no adequate understanding of the use of ceramic evidence in digging a site because, for one thing, the chronology of Attic vase painting had not yet been correctly established and, for another, stratification analysis with its carefully exact determination of the order of accumulation of the successive layers of earth and debris and artefacts had not yet become a fundamental concern for the science of excavation.

Several years passed before any effective attempt was made to evaluate the chronological evidence uncovered in this area – evidence partially recorded at the time of digging, but thereupon destroyed by a promiscuous refilling of the site. Then, in 1902, Wilhelm Dörpfeld, who had won worldwide notoriety as Schliemann's technical adviser at the site of ancient Troy, published an article entitled 'The Date of the Older Parthenon', in which he gave the first well-considered interpretation of the bearing of the excavated material on the history of the Parthenon. His results were not entirely conclusive.

Somewhat later a student of the several thousand fragments of decorated vases recovered in the excavation suggested that the findspots of many of these had been noted and recorded at the time of their uncovery with sufficient exactness to permit a reasonably reliable reconstruction of the stratification levels of the site; and actual attainment of this objective was brought in sight when two German archaeologists, Botho Graef and Ernst Langlotz, produced in 1925 and 1933 a magisterial publication of all the fragments of ancient vases recovered from the soil of the Acropolis. It remained for the great American authority on Greek architecture, William Bell Dinsmoor, to exploit this opportunity in an heroic and largely successful attempt to recover enough chronological evidence to assign limiting dates to the construction of the temple platform and to each of the five walls hidden under the modern re-terracing of the area. Many of the conclusions that he reached were highly unexpected. In order to appreciate them we must compare the two diagrams [4] and [5].

4. Parthenon substructure, cross-section at the east end

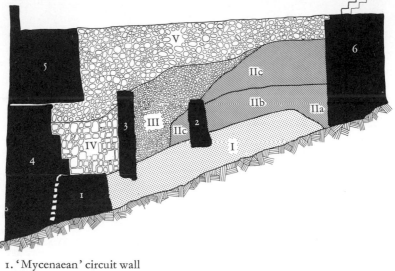

1. 'Mycenaean' circuit wall
2. Polygonal retaining wall
3. Ashlar retaining wall
4. Kimonian Acropolis wall
5. Periclean addition
6. Foundation platform of the Parthenon

It had long been known that the great platform beneath the Parthenon rested directly on native rock. To this end, the century-old accumulation of soil covering the rock must have been dug away by the builders. In addition, in order to provide the masons with working space for placing the bottom courses, a trench with gently-sloping sides had been opened along the platform's southern face. (This is the V-shaped area IIa in diagram [4] that cuts into the standing cover of older soil indicated by the Roman numeral I.) There is evidence to prove that the masonry of the platform was not lifted into place by use of scaffolding of constantly increasing height, but that. as the structure rose, the

5. Parthenon substructure, plan showing retaining walls on the south

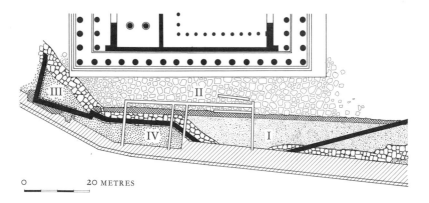

⌗ Mycenaean (1 in plan opposite)
▨ Polygonal wall (2)
■ Ashlar terrace wall (3)
▨ Kimonian–Periclean Acropolis wall (4, 5)

III II IV I

0   20 METRES

adjoining ground level was also raised abreast of it by heaping up what-ever loose soil and work-chips from dressing the stone blocks or other discardable material might be available. Consequently, as the height of the platform increased, the fill thrown in along it became an ever steeper-sloping mound. It was to prevent this loosely compacted material from washing down and spilling over the Acropolis wall that the retaining wall 2 was erected in a sort of polygonal technique (i.e. of blocks haphazardly shaped, but trimmed to fit each other's outline).

As diagram [5] shows, the course of this wall was laid approximately parallel to the platform, to create a sloping terrace about forty feet wide.

In diagram [4] (which reproduces Dinsmoor's redrawing of Dörpfeld's original design) a distinction is made between stratum IIb, forming a level terrace at about half the height of the platform, and a superposed stratum IIc that slopes down to the top of wall 2 and has spilled over it; but this is a distinction that Dinsmoor himself admits is not really discernible in the evidence. Neither is it possible to determine how high stratum II was banked up against the platform.

It is a reasonable (and, indeed, almost inescapable) inference from the situation presented in diagram [4] that the construction of the platform and the polygonal wall and the accumulation of the debris between them were closely contemporary events; and the latest datable material imbedded in stratum II should be virtually contemporary with the platform's construction.

Now, Professor Dinsmoor claimed that, whereas stratum I contained – as might have been expected – no material of later date than the sixth century B.C., stratum II included a number of vase sherds from the early fifth century, yet none that could certainly be dated later than c. 490 B.C. This crucial material evidence was examined by Professor Dinsmoor who found that the Parthenon foundation could be dated to c. 495 B.C. or a few years later. (*See* Note 2 on page 164.)

This is a conclusion of vital importance for assigning historical dates to the erection of one of the world's most famous monuments. For it signifies that the project of a great new temple for the city-goddess of Athens was initiated in (or shortly after) the year 490 B.C. because that was the very year of Athens' victorious battle against the Persian invader, in which she foiled his attempt at a beach-head landing in the Bay of Marathon and thereby postponed for a full decade the wrath of the King of Kings.

The inference from Professor Dinsmoor's observation is as reasonable as it is attractive, to the effect that the project of a new temple for the city-goddess Athena was an outcome of the victory of Marathon, and that its realization was begun by the construction of an ambitiously large and high platform to raise the new temple to the topmost elevation of Athena's citadel. Accordingly, when we read in Demosthenes (XXII, 13) that 'the Parthenon was built from the spoils of Marathon', we must understand this to mean that these were the funds with which the temple's construction was begun. Presumably, Athena's own share of the proceeds of the captured accoutrements from the battlefield provided some of the money, although popular support of the undertaking may well have brought additional contributions from private resources and the public exchequer.

Judging by the height of the fill heaped against the platform in stratum II, construction of the platform was completed in this initial campaign, and the exposed area beside it was covered with a screen of debris and earth, sloping sharply down to the polygonal retaining wall 2, probably leaving the four uppermost courses of masonry of the platform still visible (since these four courses show more carefully finished faces than the rest). But there is evidence that construction of the temple itself had also been started, even though it did not progress very far before it was violently interrupted. This evidence is still to be seen today, in the shape of a peculiar feature in the fortification wall enclosing the Acropolis. For there, in its northern sector, not far from the place where the Persians stormed the citadel in 480 B.C. and, more precisely, just to the north of the later fifth-century temple of Erechtheus, a series of large column drums of marble may be seen, solidly built into the outer face of the wall [6]. Closer inspection will reveal that most of these are *bottom* drums of columns. Largely by elimination of any other possible place for them elsewhere, they have been identified by general agreement as having been moved to their present position from previous location on the Parthenon platform. There they must have stood on the uppermost of the steps outlining a temple under construction.

It should be observed that the first stage in building a Greek temple was normally the material delineation of its plan in terms of its exterior circuit of steps with, on the top step or stylobate, a bottom drum for

6. Acropolis, bottom drums of columns built into the fortification wall

each of the columns, to fix that column's precise location. These drums were roughly shaped, undressed cylinders of solid marble with no indication of the final appearance of the column except where the drum rested on the stylobate. There, for an inch or two of height, the start of the column's twenty flutes was carefully carved as a guide for the final dressing of the entire shaft – an operation not to be performed until all the rest of the temple had been erected.

The fact that mainly *bottom* drums together with discarded step blocks of hard limestone or marble are found built into the Acropolis wall indicates that a temple plan had been laid out on its platform in the manner just described, but the work on the structure had not progressed beyond a preliminary stage. For some reason, construction of the temple had been halted.

What this reason was, is not in the least in doubt.

In the autumn of the year 480 B.C. the Athenian people fled from their endangered city, leaving only a few of the more destitute inhabitants, together with some of the priests. These barricaded themselves on the Acropolis behind wooden gates and timber shoring, while the invading Persians, as Herodotus tells the story,

encamped over against the Acropolis on the hill that the Athenians call Areopagos and thence began the siege in the following way: wrapping their arrows in tow, which they then set on fire, they shot these against the wooden hoarding, so that the besieged were betrayed by their own defences. Nevertheless, though at the very extremity of ill, they continued to hold out, so that Xerxes was long at a loss, for that he could not capture them.

At length, however, a way out of the difficulty was discovered by the barbarian. At the edge of the rock, behind the gates and the entrance ascent, where no guard was set since no one expected that any man could climb up there, some succeeded in making the ascent at the sanctuary of Cecrops' daughter Aglauros, despite the sheer steepness of the spot.

When the Athenians beheld them already up, some hurled themselves over the wall and so perished, while others sought refuge in the inner room of the temple. But the Persians who had made the ascent turned first to the gates and after they had opened these, massacred the refugees. Then, when all were laid low, they plundered the temple and fired all the hilltop.

So Xerxes was complete master of Athens.

It has been widely asserted that the column drums immured in the Acropolis north wall have at some time been damaged by fire; and as fire could not have reached them in their present location, their calcined condition is supposed to have resulted from the Persian devastation of the Acropolis. From this premise it follows further that at the time of the Persian attack, construction of a colonnaded temple had been begun on the platform beneath the existing Parthenon, but had not progressed beyond an early phase when the work was interrupted and, in consequence of serious damage inflicted by the invaders, abandoned.

That the Persian devastation of the Acropolis had indeed been as savage and as thorough as Herodotus thought became manifest to modern eyes when excavation by the Greek Service of Antiquities uncovered in 1886–7 that rich array of mutilated archaic dedicatory statues which today delight the visitor to the Acropolis museum [7 and 8]. But while it was a comparatively easy task for the Persian soldiers to overturn and shatter these statues and destroy the shrines on the hilltop, it is not equally clear that they could have subjected a series of

7. Kore,
520–510 B.C.

8. Kore, votive offering of Euthydikos,
c. 480 B.C.

marble column drums on a stone flooring to destruction by flame. It is generally suggested that the columns were enclosed in wooden scaffolding which could be set on fire and which would have generated intense enough heat. But the objection to this suggestion has been that, large wooden timbering being in scant supply in ancient Attica, a limited amount of scaffolding would have been employed and this would have been moved from one column to the next as their drums were hoisted into place, so that an entire colonnade could not have been fired as suggested. Besides, a careful count of the drums built into the Acropolis north wall, together with those of similar dimensions unearthed elsewhere on the hilltop, shows that only fourteen bottom drums have survived. It can be shown that all of these had once been set in place and that four (or perhaps five) drums of slightly smaller diameter had been set upon them, but that fifteen additional drums intended for second, third, or fourth place in a column had been made ready for use but had never been set. If these observations are substantially correct, it may be inferred that the colonnade for one of the long flanks of the temple had been laid out in terms of its bottom drums – with the apparent exception of the end columns of the series, which were to be set as belonging to the short end rows of the peristyle – and that work had been begun on the erection of some of these fourteen columns, but had made little progress at the time when the destructive Persian invasion put an abrupt end to the undertaking. Consequently, there is no reason to assume that any scaffolding had yet been erected, so that no conflagration could have occurred. Nonetheless, the existing column stumps and the steps on which they stood could have been mutilated with mallets and sledges, to make them unfit for further use.

But what plan was intended for the temple that was in process of being laid out?

On the assumption that sixteen columns were to be set on each of the long flanks – and these, if normally spaced, could very satisfactorily have been accommodated on the existing platform – the only plausible arrangement calls for six columns at front and rear. This solution depends on the calculation that eight columns at the ends of the temple would have been crowded impossibly close together on the platform, while seven columns must be excluded because an odd number at front and rear does not occur in Greek temples of the mature period for the simple reason that a column would then occupy the central axis, thereby blocking the view of the cult statue through the temple doorway.

But if this was the original design, the question arises why, in view of the tremendous outlay of material and labour incident to so ambitious an underlying foundation, a smaller platform was not constructed more in agreement with the overall size of the temple to be reared upon it. In pertinent reply diagram [9] of the substructure, which has already supplied so much information, comes to our aid. If the stratification of fill IIc has been correctly recorded there, then (as previously observed) the platform must have protruded above ground, so that it would not have been prudent or safe to bring the temple steps to the platform's edge. Either the task of heightening retaining wall 2 sufficiently to hold

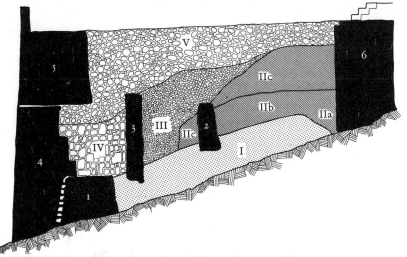

9. Parthenon substructure, cross-section at the east end

the slope flush with the platform was judged unrepaying or, more probably, there was no wish to conceal the new temple's skyward thrust above the city's rocky crown.

But, in fact, no temple was built at this time, because the Persian capture of Athens put a sudden end to the project. During the decade of the 480s, which is to say between the Greek victory at Marathon in 490 B.C. and the terrible Persian reprisal of 480–479, the great platform was built, the steps for a temple were set in place upon it, and erection of one long row of peripteral columns had been barely begun. Then all further work was suspended as a result of the Persian destruction of the city.

Despite the naval victory off the island of Salamis and the total defeat of the Persian land forces at Plataea, the plight of the Athenians was pitiable. W. Judeich in *Topographie von Athen* gives this vivid description of the city after the departure of the Persians:

When the Athenians returned to their homes in the winter of 479 they found a rubble heap in place of a town. Save for a few brief stretches, the walls of the city had been destroyed; the houses, built entirely of fieldstone and mudbrick, lay in utter ruin; shrines and temples had been burnt and their dedications either broken up or carried off . . . An entire new city had to be built. Yet, thanks to the enormous political and economic revival of Athens after the war, this task was relatively soon accomplished. During the fifty years that intervened between the Persian and the Peloponnesian wars, Athens experienced its most brilliant architectural period. The controlling power may have been vested in the city council and so, in final analysis in the body of the people itself; but the true arbiters and fashioners of the new city were the great statesmen who guided the destiny of Athens by virtue of their personal ascendancy, now working together, now in opposition to one another – Themistocles, Kimon, Pericles. In comparison with these, other outstanding citizens, of whom there was no lack in that great period, were of only minor account.

To revert to the immediate aftermath of the Persian retreat, the most urgent task for the shelterless and defenceless Athenians on reoccupying their ravaged city was to rebuild their houses and repair and extend their protecting city wall. Thucydides, in an early chapter of his *History*, gives an account of this latter enterprise and how it was accomplished in circumvention of Spartan diplomatic attempts to prevent the fortification of a city already sensed as a potential adversary to Spartan military supremacy. The passage in the *History* begins:

After the barbarians had departed from the land, the Athenian citizenry at once began transporting their children and womenfolk and surviving possessions back from their place of refuge and started rebuilding the city and its walls. For only short stretches of the circuit remained standing and most of the private houses were in ruins (although some few had survived, in which the Persian commanders had lodged).

There follows an account of the delaying *pourparlers* with Sparta, after which Thucydides continues his narrative:

And so in this way the Athenians walled their city in brief time; and even today it is apparent that the building was performed in haste. For, the foundations are laid of all kinds of stone, in some places not even trimmed to fit, but brought up just as they were; and many upright tombstones and wrought marble slabs have been built in. For, the circuit of the city was everywhere increased and on this account they laid hands on anything and everything in their haste.

Nowhere does Thucydides make any mention of a new temple for Athena under construction at the time of the Persian invasion or in the succeeding years preceding Pericles' rise to power; neither does any other ancient author or surviving inscription make any similar reference. In consequence, modern opinion has held that no immediate attempt was made to repair the Persian damage by resuming work on the Parthenon. For thirty years (it is asserted) the platform stood idle and empty while no effort was made to provide the city's guardian goddess with a proper dwelling-place.

But such a proposition is extremely improbable. It becomes completely incredible when the material evidence against it is properly examined and impartially reviewed.

Once again it is the buried walls south of the Parthenon from which we must derive, if we can, some understanding of events that took place nearly two thousand five hundred years ago. It is the ashlar retaining wall (3 on [4]) on which the argument depends. This wall can be shown to date from the late 470s or early 460s (*see* Note 3 on page 165) and since its construction argues a resumption of building activity on the temple platform we must assume that work on a temple was under way at least twenty years before Pericles succeeded Kimon in 449 B.C. and initiated the present Parthenon, with Iktinos as its master-builder, in 447 B.C.

Much the same conclusion may be reached from careful consideration of an otherwise baffling and disappointing historic document. Annual statements of receipts and disbursements in connexion with the construction of the Periclean Parthenon were rendered by the Treasurers of Athena and the Treasurers of the Public Funds (known as the *Hellenotamiai*). These summary accounts were engraved on the four faces of a thin upright marble slab which, in the course of centuries, was broken into minute disordered fragments. Some ten per cent of these small pieces have been recovered (Epigraphical Museum, Athens) and with great ingenuity and patience reassembled and assigned appropriate positions in an imaginary reconstitution of the shattered monument. A probable, but extremely incoherent text results, comprising a great many incomplete numerical notations of money received and expended, together with still more fragmentary indications of the purposes for which the various amounts were paid.

The accounts cover the fifteen years between 447 and 432 B.C.; but in the last five years of this period there were no disbursements for the Parthenon except in connexion with sculpture for the pediments. It appears certain that in all other respects the temple was complete by 438 B.C., during which year surplus material was sold publicly (there is mention of wood, probably from scaffolding such as had been erected for carving the famous frieze and for decorating in colour the marble ceiling coffers). For the preceding year of 439–438 there is mention of

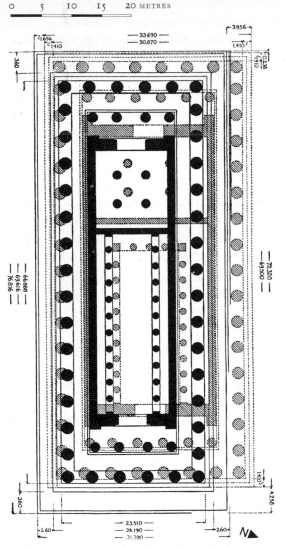

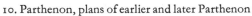

10. Parthenon, plans of earlier and later Parthenon

Black: Kallikrates' plan (earlier)
Shaded: Iktinos' plan (later)

purchase of ivory and payments made to woodworkers and gilders; and it is presumed that these items refer to the final decoration and adornment of the completed structure. The great doors of the temple are included in the very fragmentary record of the next earlier year (440–439) – again suggesting a closing phase of the work; and two years before that (442–441), the word for columns occurs without legible context. Yet the only plausible reference must be to the final fluting of the columns, since their erection was always the earliest stage of Greek temple construction and, once the columns were in place, no further work on them was undertaken until all the rest of the structure had been completed. From all these considerations it would follow with almost entire certainty that, apart from the final detail of the surface dressing of the marble and the application of colouring, the Periclean Parthenon took only five years to build!

Yet, it is physically impossible that such a massive and magnificent structure of perfectly cut and fitted marble could have been produced in so short a space of time with no materials more immediately available than the marble-veined mid-height of Mt Pentelikon, eleven miles away.

It is now more than fifty years since the late B. H. Hill published his brilliant paper, 'The Older Parthenon', in which he deduced the ground plan [10] of an earlier temple set out and partly erected on much the same foundation as the present Parthenon. Having observed that a corner block from a range of steps for some earlier building lies behind the bottom step of the present temple, Hill succeeded in proving that this earlier stepblock had never been moved from its present position and that it was one of an entire range of similar stepblocks lying behind the bottom step of the present Parthenon's south flank. Moreover, these earlier steps likewise belonged to the bottom step of their flight. Since the corner stepblock was still in place, it fixed the location of the older temple's corner column at this (the south-west) end of the building; and the discovery of discarded marble blocks from the top step of the same flight, showing setting marks for columns, revealed the base diameter of these columns. From this information, combined with the known dimensions of the platform and the inferred dimensions of the area defined by the temple steps, Hill was able to calculate that sixteen columns were intended for the flanks and six for the ends. The remaining elements of the plan were deduced partly from other discarded blocks and partly from a presumed resemblance to the interior arrangement of the present Parthenon.

All in all, it was a remarkable achievement, illustrating Hill's unequalled acuity of observation and technical understanding of Greek architectural practice. What is perhaps even more remarkable is that Hill's conclusions have never been seriously challenged.

The resulting temple plan is presented in drawing [10] superimposed in solid black on the existing Parthenon at identical scale. It is instantly apparent that the two temples have much in common.

Except that the Later Parthenon is slightly longer (by a single

11. Parthenon, east colonnade, view from within

column) and noticeably wider (by two columns), the later plan reproduces the earlier in almost every detail. In both, shallow porticoes with free-standing columns are set at either end of the interior sanctuary, itself divided into two rooms by a closed partition wall. The chamber at the rear is relatively small, with depth equal to or less than the width; whereas the other compartment, accessible through a wide doorway opening off the front portico, is much greater in length and has rows of interior columns dividing it into a wide nave with narrow aisles. Accordingly, the later plan reproduces the essential disposition of the earlier one in an expanded form.

But it is remarkable that this increase in overall size is not accompanied by any proportionate increment in the constituent elements of the structure: the new walls are no thicker, the columns no stouter, the exterior flight of steps no broader and hence presumably no higher [11

12. Parthenon, exterior view of east colonnade

and 12]. Actually, the column diameters are identical, although the interval at which the columns are spaced, instead of being greater, is less by $4\frac{1}{2}$ inches (0·115 metres). And unless some change in architectural tradition occurred during the brief time separating the making of

13. Parthenon, triglyph and geison in north-west corner

the two plans, this near-identity of dimensions in the external colonnade must have led to an equally close agreement in the dimensions of every one of the constituent elements of the superstructure – that is to say, in architectural parlance, the Doric entablature with its epistyle, or architrave; its frieze of alternating triglyphs and metopes; its geison, or cornice [13]; and its sima, or roof trough. However, as I shall shortly have reason to emphasize, it is readily calculable that a shrinking of the column interval by 4½ inches (0·115 metres) would entail a proportionate diminution in the width of every metope by nearly 2 inches (0·051 metres).

It is hardly arguable that this very extraordinary procedure of enlarging the size of a temple without any corresponding increase in the dimensions of its component elements was due to the restrictive area of the platform. For the length of the platform was sufficient to accommodate seventeen slightly larger columns at slightly greater intervals; while, in order to permit an increase in the temple's width from six to eight columns, some sort of supplementary extension of the platform on the north side was unavoidable. We must seek some other explanation why so many of the dimensions of the structural elements of the earlier temple were kept unaltered in the later one.

If plan [10] is scrutinized closely, the platform may be identified as the outermost rectangle delineated by solid line. (The broken dotted lines describe the exterior steps of the Later Parthenon; and the *inner* series of solid lines gives the plan of the older temple.) With these identifications in mind, it will be seen that the smaller earlier temple is symmetrically centred on the platform, whereas the existing Parthenon is not.

As laid out in the ground plan, an open walk or freeway surrounded the older temple between its lowest step and the platform's verge, leaving a space nearly 12 feet (3·60 metres) wide at either end of the temple and one of 8½ feet (2·60 metres) along either flank. In marked contrast the present Parthenon is placed on the platform without regard to symmetrical disposition, as is clearly shown in plan [10]. On the west (i.e. at the upper end of the plan) the temple steps extend along the very border of the platform (shown in solid line); whereas at the other or eastern end the platform stretches 14 feet (4·26 metres) beyond the temple steps, and on the south (at the left of the plan) the open space beyond the bottom step measures barely $5\frac{1}{2}$ feet (1·68 metres). These relationships between the extant Parthenon and the platform are distinguishable in diagram [4]; but for the north side the plan [10] must again be consulted. There the colonnade of the present Parthenon has been carried far out beyond the platform upon newly added masonry with its bed at the east cut down into the living rock of the Acropolis. There could be no more convincing proof that platform and earlier temple were conceived as integral parts of a single design and that the present Parthenon was an intruder upon a differently intended project.

Yet several questions arise that have not hitherto been satisfactorily answered, notably 'Whose project was this Older Parthenon?' and 'How much of it was ever actually built?'

Hill believed that he had recovered the plan for the temple under construction at the time of the Persian invasion and abruptly abandoned after the Persian sack of the city and its citadel when (according to Herodotus) Mardonius, the Persian commander, 'retreated from Attica after having set fire to Athens and overturned and demolished everything still standing – city walls, private dwellings, sanctuaries'. But it now appears – from the evidence we have just deduced from the retaining walls and fills [4] – that the plan so ingeniously elicited by Hill was not that of the pre-Persian project (which may, or again may not, have been the same), but reproduces the plan of a temple in course of construction *after* the departure of the Persians.

If now we turn to the second of the questions previously formulated and ask how much of this 'Kimonian Parthenon' was ever completed, there might seem to be little prospect of finding an acceptable answer. Yet there are several indications (albeit of a rather technical nature) to assist our inquiry. They are not too difficult to follow, provided that the reader takes an interest in, and has no distaste, but rather a liking for, the minutiae of Greek architectural detail.

Built into the foundation support under the marble floor of the present Parthenon, as a filler in lieu of a more ordinary flagstone, there lies a marble slab with edges carved to the profile shown in [14]. Six

14. Older Parthenon, wallbase moulding

15. Hephaisteion (Theseion), wallbase moulding

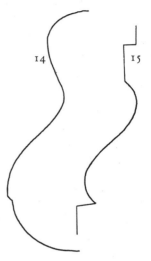

14

15

other blocks carrying the same profile have been built inside the Parthenon west wall. All seven of these must be discarded material from some nearby source and, there being no other possibility, must have originally belonged to the Kimonian Parthenon. The block now under the temple floor has been identified as an end block (anta base) for the sanctuary wall of the earlier Parthenon and on examination shows cuttings for the iron clamps by which it was formerly held in place. The other six blocks with identical profile moulding once formed part of the stepped base of the same wall.

Now it is normal in the *Ionic* Order for such a wall to carry a profiled base responding to that of the exterior Ionic columns. But because Doric columns do not have a base, there was no logical reason for setting a profiled base at the foot of the sanctuary wall of a Doric building. It might therefore be objected that these blocks, with a profile suggesting that of the well-known Attic-Ionic column base, could not have come from the earlier Parthenon because floormarks for the columns of this temple prove beyond dispute that they were Doric. Yet the Doric Hephaisteion (popularly known as the Theseion), which dates from the period immediately after the construction of the Kimonian Parthenon was halted, has a moulded wallbase with a strikingly similar profile [15]. The inference is clear: the architect who designed the Kimonian Parthenon (whom we shall have reason to identify as Kallikrates) favoured this Ionic feature for his Doric temple, as did also the architect of the Hephaisteion; whereas the architect of the Later Parthenon (for whom we shall accept the well attested name Iktinos) rejected and discarded this Ionic element as inappropriate to a building in the Doric style.

But that is not all!

From the presence of cuttings for horizontal clamps and the absence of cuttings for vertical dowels on the profiled base under the Parthenon floor, Hill deduced that the moulded base for the sanctuary wall of the earlier Parthenon had previously been set in place, but that the wall itself had not been erected. But on the strength of an observation made during the recent exploration of the foundations of the Hephaisteion, to the effect that there the entire exterior colonnade was erected before any of the other elements of the plan were laid out, it should follow for the nearly contemporary Kimonian Parthenon that, since construction of the inner sanctuary had begun, the outer colonnade should have already been completed at the time when work on the temple ceased – in other words, the columns were already standing!

If we ask why construction was thus brought to a halt, the answer can only be that it was because of the intervention of Pericles in 448 B.C. with a new and more ambitious plan, with Iktinos replacing Kallikrates as master-builder in charge.

In support of this hypothesis of a mid fifth-century date for the earlier Parthenon it may be argued that the moulded wallbase on which the discussion relies could not have been introduced into the structure damaged by the Persians because firstly, its presence there would have implied the previous erection of the exterior colonnade, whereas the discarded drums attributed to this project show (by latest count) only twenty-three drums had been set in place with all but four or five of these assured as bottom drums, while some further material for columns had been brought from the quarries but not yet used; and secondly, the profile of the wallbase has no parallel in early fifth-century architecture, whereas it so closely resembles the wallbase of the Hephaisteion [15] (begun around the middle of the century) and so definitely anticipates the canonic Attic–Ionic column base of the Propylaea [33 :B] (begun in 437 B.C.) and the Erechtheion [33 :C, D] (begun a decade or so later) that its invention must be attributed to c. 460–450 B.C. many years later than the Persian invasion.

On the currently prevailing view that the temple plan retrieved by Hill [10] represents a project which had been undertaken *before* the Persian invasion but which had never been completed beyond setting the circuit of steps and the start of some of the columns, it has always seemed strange – and indeed inexplicable – that the Periclean Parthenon kept precisely the same base dimensions for its columns (and presumably much the same height) even while it set them a trifle nearer together. But now a simple and straightforward explanation presents itself. The columns of the later Parthenon had the identical dimensions of the earlier ones because *they were the same columns*, having been dismounted and then re-erected.

That the Parthenon columns belong to an older generation of Athenian architecture is suggested by their thickness in relation to their height. Demonstrably there was a continuous trend in favour of more slender columns during the fifth and fourth centuries B.C.; and if we interpolate the Parthenon columns into the series of Athenian buildings of fifth-century date, we see that they should antedate the Hephaisteion (*c.* 449–444 B.C.) by an appreciable interval.

The series runs as follows:

Temple	Date	Ratio of bottom diameter of column to its height*
Parthenon	?	5·48
Hephaisteion	449–444	5·61
Ares	444–440?	5·70
Sunium, Poseidon II	440–436?	5·78
Rhamnus	436–432?	5·74
Propylaea, east façade	437–432	5·48 (copying Parthenon)
Delos, Temple of Athenians	425–417	5·71

Furthermore, the height of the exterior columns of the Parthenon reproduces exactly that of the exterior columns of the temple of Zeus at Olympia, erected during the decade of the 460s. Now, it is extremely unlikely that this dimension should have been copied in Athens by a Periclean architect, whereas it might well have impressed a contemporary Kimonian builder to imitation.

It has been objected that once a column had been set up it could not again be moved, because the projecting bosses for the lifting tackle would have been trimmed off, leaving no place for securing ropes around the drums. I very much doubt the correctness of this assertion. In the 1920s when the fallen columns of the north flank were re-erected by the Greek Service of Antiquities under supervision of the late Nicholas Balanos no difficulty was experienced in either lowering or raising the column drums, and this too although the columns had been fluted (as would not have been the case for the columns of the unfinished earlier Parthenon).

If one takes account of the great outlay of time, money and labour for quarrying a new set of drums on Mt Pentelikon, for sliding them

* Dates and ratios from William Bell Dinsmoor's *Architecture of Ancient Greece.*

48

with snubbing ropes down the mountainside, for loading them on carts drawn by teams of oxen and transporting them ten miles to the city and drawing them up with winches over laid timbers to the plateau level of the Acropolis, and there trimming them to proper dimensions for use, it will be appreciated that the saving effected by re-using drums already correctly graded, trimmed and fitted, and immediately available, can hardly be overestimated.

But if we subscribe to this new proposition that the columns of the earlier building supplied the material for the later one, we are immediately confronted by what seems to be a formidable difficulty: why did Iktinos not leave the columns where they stood, instead of giving himself all the trouble of dismounting and re-erecting them – only to move them a very short distance? Closer study of the two ground plans combined in [16] will yield the answer.

It will be seen that in the later scheme the count of columns has been increased from six to eight at the front and rear, and from sixteen to seventeen on the sides. This substitution of an eight by seventeen for

16. Parthenon, plans of earlier and later Parthenon

Black: Kallikrates' plan (earlier)
Shaded: Iktinos' plan (later)

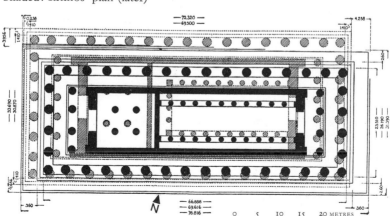

a six by sixteen columned plan, while it called for only six more columns in all, nevertheless caused serious difficulties in accommodating the enlarged structure to the platform.

The revised Parthenon, then, was to have eight columns instead of six at front and rear. The increase to eight columns, rather than to seven or nine, was dictated by the demand that the central axial vista through the doorways should be kept unobstructed. But the change from sixteen to seventeen columns on the flanks appears to have had no other motive than the canonic tradition of employing an odd number of columns on the long sides in opposition to the even number at the ends and applying a formula (whose precise explanation remains obscure to us) whereby the count of the columns on the flanks was calculated as one more than twice the number of columns on the ends.

By the time of Pericles' accession to power at the middle of the fifth century the six by sixteen plan, previously intended for the Parthenon, would have become outmoded; but this can scarcely have been the reason for the drastic and costly change to the more canonic eight by seventeen. A more plausible explanation may be found in Pericles' sponsorship of a colossal gold and ivory statue of the temple goddess, to be the work of his protegé the sculptor Pheidias and of such a size that it could not have been fitly housed in the earlier Parthenon. And yet, cogent as this suggestion is, there were still more powerful forces compelling the change in the temple plan, as will in due course be made apparent.

However this may have been, the immediate problem was how to remodel the existing and only partially completed building to fit the new and more ambitious plan.

There were various reasons why the already erected columns could not be left in place on the south flank or on either of the ends. If the extra column for the flank had merely been added to the existing row, at either end of the series, the flight of steps would have projected beyond the platform at the end, so that the temple platform would have had to be built out farther to accommodate and support them. But another consideration seems to have weighed even more heavily. As Hill succeeded in proving, the bottom step of the earlier Parthenon had not been laid in marble, as might have been expected, but in grey limestone from a nearby quarry at the base of Mt Hymettos. This seems a strange incongruity, inasmuch as the two higher steps were undoubtedly of marble. Yet the architect of the Hephaisteion had followed the same tradition (if tradition it may be called), as any visitor to that much visited temple may still see today. Seemingly, Iktinos did not approve; but instead of tearing the step out (which would have entailed the total dismantling of steps and colonnade), he conceived the ingenious and highly practical solution of coating the three Kimonian steps with a new flight of marble, setting the new steps in front of, and level with, the old ones. The only inconvenience resulting from this alteration was the necessity of moving all the columns forward, since in a Greek temple the peristyle runs flush with the outer edge of the top step and this top step (or stylobate) had now been extended.

And because the columns of the southern flank had all to be taken down in order to be moved to their new position, Iktinos took advantage of this occasion to re-erect them slightly closer together. It has been calculated that whereas the present Parthenon's columns are set at an average interval of 14 feet (4·295 metres to be exact), the columns of the earlier temple were set slightly more than 4 inches (0·105 metres) farther apart – seemingly a negligible difference, yet adding up in a row of seventeen columns to more than five feet. But what was Iktinos' purpose in making this small correction?

From [17] (which omits the earlier temple) it will be seen that on the west, at the rear of the temple, Iktinos moved the steps with their range of columns to the extreme edge of the platform, thereby gaining an equivalent amount of platform space at the east along the temple front. From [16] (which gives both plans) it will be evident that on the north the widened Parthenon could not all be carried on the platform, but

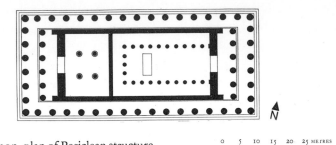

17. Parthenon, plan of Periclean structure

O   5   10   15   20   25 METRES

demanded additional foundations for its row of seventeen columns with their flight of steps. That such addition had indeed been made may easily be verified today by examining the northern portion of the west end of the temple, where the foundations stand exposed to view [18]. It does not take a professionally schooled eye to appreciate from the run of the joints in the masonry that new blocks have been bonded-in to extend the underpinning for the present steps and columns here

18. Parthenon, foundations at the north-west corner

at the north-west corner of the Parthenon. But [16] fails to show in a comprehensible manner how the surface level of the Acropolis rock rises continuously from west to east along the northern edge of the platform, with the result that, while several courses of foundation blocks had to be laid for the western half of the north flank, at the east the levelling course beneath the bottom step could be bedded directly on native rock. Had the temple extended farther towards the east, a considerable depth of living rock would have had to be quarried out. This may explain why Iktinos moved the Parthenon as far to the west as the platform permitted and, in addition, shortened its overall length by nearly 6 feet (1·79 metres) by drawing the columns a few inches closer together. Also, there would have been the further gain of 2½ feet (0·76 metres) less width of new foundation to be built under the north steps and colonnade.

In addition to the columns there would have been considerable material available for re-use, such as the blocks of the inner row of steps which, at front and rear, led up to the columned vestibules and, on the flanks, were a footing for the walls of the inner rooms. In his classic article 'The Older Parthenon', Hill had acutely observed that

the lower step of the cella of the present Parthenon is composed in large part of re-used blocks from the earlier temple as is shown by the fact that they have two sets of clamp cuttings. . . . Now the blocks thus proved to have been put to an earlier use are on the average 1·77 m. long. This is a standard length (six Solonian feet) in the substructure of the Older Parthenon, but it is not normal for the present Parthenon. It is, however, the average length of twenty of the twenty-nine blocks of the lower step of the north side of the cella and of a number on the other sides. All these had doubtless been used in the older Parthenon.

The Kimonian Parthenon had topped these steps along the flank with a profiled wallbase [14] which Iktinos discarded, utilizing some of its blocks for filling underneath the floor of the sanctuary and within the walls, where they have survived to the present day.

There are other anomalies in the Parthenon, such as would not be probable in a wholly new building. Thus, the columns that frame the front portico are more slender than the corresponding ones of the rear – and the diameter of this latter set is identical with some exceptionally small drums immured in the Acropolis north wall. On this and other evidence Hill declared that 'when the present Parthenon was planned, it was made in many dimensions precisely the same as the older temple, so that blocks from the latter, not too much injured, might be used in the new building'.

But it strains all credulity to believe what Hill and many others have maintained, that so much excellent and costly material, previously assembled, had somehow escaped the wanton destructiveness of the Persians, only to lie untouched and idle through thirty years while Athena waited in vain for a fitting shrine and Athens grew rich and great, yet nothing was done until at last Pericles intervened to build a temple for the city's patron goddess on the platform that had stood ready but useless for three decades.

However, there is no need to entertain so improbable an hypothesis, since the evidence that I have reviewed shows that an earlier Parthenon was in course of construction during the period of Kimon's ascendancy, which lasted with only brief interruption from the death of Aristides in 468 B.C. until Kimon's own death in 450. It was then that Pericles, putting Iktinos in charge of the altered project for the temple, substituted for the Kimonian Parthenon the more ambitious and considerably more costly building, whose impressive remains still stand after 2,500 years.

A more difficult task than proving the existence of a partially completed Kimonian Parthenon is that of determining how much of it had actually been built before Pericles halted it. Granted the validity of Hill's claim that 'when the present Parthenon was planned, it was made in many dimensions precisely the same as the older temple, so that blocks from the latter might be used in the new building', it is this very identity of dimensions that seems to preclude any possibility of distinguishing between old and new material in the present temple. Perhaps something more can be made of the intriguing clue of the altered foot-rule; but if so, it will demand some highly ingenious manipulation of the available measurements. As matters stand, the search for Kimonian survivals in the extant ruined temple has been a frustrating occupation. It is true, of course, that the slightly diminished column interval necessitated an equal abbreviation of the architrave beams, if these were re-used; but this would leave no discoverable trace on the marble blocks. An equivalent curtailment would have been necessary in the frieze, if any of the alternating triglyph and metope blocks had been cut and carved preparatory to setting in place. But here again the re-use of these pieces might not be detectable, since two or three inches might be trimmed from the border of each of the metopes and the triglyphs would not have to be recut. If the work were done carefully and the sculptured reliefs were not mutilated, no trace of the operation would be visible.

And yet there was one feature of the metopes that no change of measurements could alter and no resetting could obscure. That persisting feature was the sculptural style of the metope reliefs.

No visitor to the British Museum who examines the Elgin Marbles with any attention to their artistic qualities will fail to be struck by the lack of stylistic harmony between the metopes [19, 20, 21 and 22] on the one hand and the pedimental statues [23 and 24] and the wall-frieze [25] on the other. So great is the naturalistic advance in rendering anatomic detail and posing figures in action and so fully developed are the aesthetic devices for representing drapery on the Panathenaic gathering in the frieze and on the surviving statues from the two pediments, that no technical diversity of medium between low relief and high, or again between high relief and figures in the round, can mitigate or

19. Parthenon, metope, Lapith and Centaur

20. Parthenon, metope, Lapith and Centaur

explain away the semi-archaic severity and anatomic rigidity displayed on the metopes. The contrast of style is too pronounced to be due to mere variety of manner among contemporary sculptural workshops, but betokens an interval of a full artistic generation measurable at some twenty years.

21. Parthenon, metope, Lapith and Centaur

Students of Greek sculpture have long been aware of this stylistic discrepancy and are wholly at a loss to explain it. Yet the explanation is surprisingly simple and entirely convincing: the existing metopes showing the contest of Lapiths and Centaurs *were carved for the Kimonian Parthenon.*

22. Parthenon, metope, Lapith and Centaur

23. Parthenon, figures from the east pediment

24. Parthenon, figure from the east pediment

25. Parthenon, detail of frieze

A second criterion, complementary to that of sculptural style, confirms the Kimonian origin of these metopes.

When viewed from below, the metopes of a Doric temple appear to fit snugly against the triglyphs that frame them [26 and 27]; but actually the metopes are a few inches broader than they seem and extend behind the face of the triglyph into a narrow vertical slot cut in the triglyph

26. Parthenon, entablature at south-west corner

27. Parthenon, metope at south-west corner

block. This overlap, amounting to no more than a couple of inches at each end of the slab, secures the metope in place. It will naturally be smooth and blank, lest any of the carved relief be hidden.

Because the Kimonian column span had been shortened by about $4\frac{1}{2}$ inches (o·115 metres) in the Periclean version, any metope from the older structure would have proved oversize for the later one by half this amount, or a trifle more than 2 inches (·057 metres) (on the assumption that the Kimonian triglyphs were not made correspondingly narrower or new ones substituted). Therefore, the older metopes would either have had to be discarded entirely or else cut down to a suitable size. It is scarcely surprising that the latter alternative was chosen, since it was a minor task to cut off a couple of inches of marble in comparison with the expense and loss of time involved in carving a new set of metopes.

The fact that the sculptured reliefs on these metopes were stylistically behind the times and must have seemed old-fashioned with their rigid poses and arbitrary compositional patterns did not count heavily enough to warrant their total rejection. Instead, they were relegated to the temple's least frequently visited and least adequately viewable southern flank.

Had the reduction of the metopes to the narrower width been done carefully, the operation would have left no discernible trace. But fortunately for our modern interest in architectural history, the work was done hastily and crudely – a sure indication that the work was done 'on the job' in the course of fitting the metopes into place. They would never have been delivered from the sculptors' shop in this condition, whereas the masons whose task it was to set them in the frieze were well aware that, once these metopes had been lowered into the triglyph slots, no one would know whether their edges were rough or smooth.

The visitor who examines the metopes in the British Museum will see that more than half of them have one or both of their end surfaces rudely cut [21 and 22]. If he is somewhat more closely observant, he will further discover that on four metopes small portions of the reliefs have been cut away at the border with consequent loss of the centaur's tail in two instances and, in another, an undercutting of his hindquarter so that the chamfered edge of a triglyph could be fitted in behind it. The centaur's tail has been shaved in [21] and on the metope shown on [22]; and on still another [20] the Lapith's drapery has been worked down to allow the triglyph to project over it (*see* Note 4, page 168).

Barely more than half of the thirty-two metopes on the south flank of the temple have survived (fifteen in the British Museum, one in the Louvre, one in the Acropolis Museum and one still *in situ* on the Parthenon). Fortunately, however, a series of drawings made by Jacques Carrey, before the disastrous explosion in 1687, records the entire series as they appeared on the temple [28]. Twenty-four of them

28. Parthenon, drawings by Jacques Carrey of south metopes, 1674

represented Lapiths and Centaurs and were so disposed that half were grouped together at the west end and half at the east end, with an intervening group of eight representing different subjects and carved in the more advanced style of the Periclean period. Compare the cramped style of the upper row (Kimonian) with the freer movement and more naturalistic drapery of the lower row (Periclean).

From the foregoing evidence we are entitled to conclude that only twenty-four carved metopes were finished and ready for the Kimonian Parthenon at the time that the Periclean project was substituted for it. Now, it is a simple calculation that the earlier Parthenon with six by sixteen columns would have required ten metopes for each façade and thirty for each of the flanks; so that the twenty-four finished metopes would have been too numerous for the two façades, yet not sufficient for the frieze of either of the flanks. Moreover, to judge from the surviving specimens, these metopes were not all produced together at any one time but, if we grant the validity of dating them on the criterion of sculptural style, they were produced over a period of more than a decade, from the mid 460s to the late 450s. It would therefore appear that the sculptors' workshops had been commissioned in advance to carve metopes in anticipation of the time when building should have progressed far enough to allow them to be set in place on the temple. Since the number of accumulated finished metopes was not sufficient for the frieze on either of the long sides of the Kimonian Parthenon, it is highly probable that none of them had been placed in position and that, consequently, the Kimonian project had not advanced beyond the erection of the peristyle columns and the start of building up the sanctuary walls, when all further construction was suspended as the new Periclean project supervened. There must, however, have been a very considerable accumulation of marble building material, rough shaped or in course of preparation for use, in the workshops on the site. Like the metopes, all this was available for the present Parthenon, even though with the change of plan and probable new specifications for proportions there would have been need – as shown in the case of the finished metopes – of recutting and adaptation [compare 20 and 21].

The evidence is now in. When duly weighed and evaluated, it admits no other conclusions than those advanced in the course of this study. These conclusions may be combined into three basic propositions to the effect that:

1. In or shortly after 490 B.C. a temple for Athena was projected on the Acropolis. A high stone platform to carry the temple-to-be was erected. The bottom drums for one colonnade had been laid out by 480 B.C. when the Persian invasion intervened. These bottom drums were dispersed, together with other building materials assembled on the site, during or after the Persian invasion. This projected temple is that generally known as the 'Older Parthenon'.

2. Between c. 468 and 465 B.C., under the initiative of Kimon, the leading Athenian statesman of the period, a new temple to Athena was projected on the same site and following the same plan as that of the 'Older Parthenon'. The supervising master-builder is to be identified as Kallikrates. This temple was begun and carried rather less than half way to completion when all work on it was peremptorily halted by Pericles on his assumption of political control after Kimon's death in 450 B.C.

3. At this stage a third temple on the same site, but on an enlarged plan, was projected. Kallikrates was dismissed from office and replaced by Iktinos, who was commissioned to design and build a new temple on a more impressive scale, utilizing whatever material from the unfinished building could be turned to account. This temple was completed structurally by 438 B.C. The pediment sculptures were completed by 432 B.C. This is the temple the ruins of which still stand on the Acropolis.

But why should Pericles have made such a drastic change? Was it merely in order to fit a new statue of Athena? Or to 'correct', according to mid fifth-century eyes, the over-elongated proportions of the earlier six by sixteen column temple? Such explanations have been suggested, on the assumption, of course, that the previous temple had never advanced beyond a few bottom drums of the colonnade and that a substitution of plan would therefore not be difficult or costly. But in fact, as we have just seen, the true situation was very different. Pericles intervened to put an end to an architectural undertaking in mid career and proceeded to dismantle it and rebuild it on wholly different lines.

I can think of no adequate explanation for so drastic and brutal an act unless it is derived from the violent antagonisms of Greek party politics which – while rather less extreme in Athens than in some of the other city-states of the period – threatened to erupt into violent shifts of power accompanied by inordinate acts of vengeance and counter-revenge.

During the period in which the earlier Parthenon was actively under construction, Kimon and Pericles were the statesmen guiding the two most powerful and implacably opposed factions of the Athenian citizenry in their unremitting rivalry for political control over the state and its island empire. In order to appreciate the bitter intensity of their relations to one another and the repercussions which politics may have had on the fortunes of the temple being built to honour the city's guardian goddess, we must now turn from architectural to human history.

2: Kimon and Pericles

The bitter rivalry, jealousy and personal hatred which were to mark the political careers of Kimon and Pericles probably began in their early youth. Their rivalry certainly had all the appearance – and all the ferocity – of a family vendetta. For Kimon's father, Miltiades, had been impeached by Xanthippos, the father of Pericles, and subjected to a very heavy fine after the failure of his clandestine expedition against the island of Paros in 488 B.C. Moreover, this fine was inherited by Kimon who had to pay it off after his father's death. Kimon did not, however, immediately inherit his father's political influence and power. It was not until 468 B.C., on the death of Aristides, that he gained the leading position in the aristocratic party – the party then dominant in Athenian politics in opposition to the popular party of which Pericles was to become the chief spokesman and leader.

Kimon's remarkable military talents had already been demonstrated during Aristides' lifetime by a highly successful punitive campaign in Thrace and as commander of an Attic fleet in the Hellespont and Sea of Marmara, a post to which Aristides had been deputed but which, being never addicted to the sea, he ceded to his more warlike lieutenant. But it was after Aristides' death that Kimon's military renown reached its height, in exploits never to be equalled by any Athenian on sea or land.

In a celebrated campaign against the Persian power in Asia Minor he closed with the enemy fleet off the mouth of the river Eurymedon at the head of the Pamphylian Gulf, near modern Turkish Antalya. After completely annihilating his opponent by sea, he landed his forces on the nearby coast without pausing to recover from the stress of battle, and in a bitterly contested struggle not merely gained the upper hand, but utterly routed the attendant Persian armed forces and plundered their camp, securing from the combined engagement a tremendous booty. It may be remembered that it was from the consequent enrichment of the Athenian treasury that the funds were drawn for constructing the great south wall of the Acropolis, to which the preceding chapter made repeated reference.

The precise date of the famous battle is not certain, but is very generally set at 467 or 466 B.C. By that time – to judge from the relative chronology of the supporting terrace walls south of the Parthenon and the stylistically oldest of the Centaur and Lapith metopes – construction of Athena's temple had already begun. But the new wealth in the public treasury may well have stimulated progress by supplying funds for fresh marble from the Pentelic quarries and for an increased number of stonecutters, masons and mechanics. On this, of course, we have no direct information.

Additional resources became available after 463 B.C. when Kimon was again active on a naval expedition, directed this time to the north Aegean against the island of Thasos, which had seceded from the Delian League after Athens had made it into an empire under her sway. Kimon's hard-won victory over the beleaguered opponent not only restored an important member to the alliance but gave Athens access to the fabulously rich gold mines of neighbouring southern Thrace that Thasos had been working for herself.

It should not be assumed that his military successes were alone responsible for Kimon's position of influence and power over Athenian public affairs. The leading personality in the aristocratic faction was dependent on that faction's maintenance of its authority; and this in turn was achieved by partisan favour of the supreme lawcourt of Athens, the Council of the Areopagos. Aristotle in his treatise on *The Constitution of the Athenians* states:

After the Persian wars the Council of the Areopagos regained its previous power and won control of the state. . . . Its authority was recognized and the Athenians governed themselves during this period.

Elsewhere in the same treatise we are told:

The Council of the Areopagites had the task of watching over the laws; in fact, it supervised the largest and most important part of the life of the community in that it had final authority over fining and punishing offenders.

The composition of the court inclined its members to act in favour of the Kimonian aristocratic faction. For these were all ex-magistrates of the annually elected office of archons; and inasmuch as only the wealthier classes of citizens were eligible for archonship, the orientation of the court in sympathy with the aristocratic party of Kimon was firmly assured. As Aristotle recorded:

The selection of the archons was based on distinction of birth and wealth; and it was from the archons that the Areopagites were recruited.

Against this aristocratic stranglehold on the administration of public affairs the only effective countermove available to the opposite faction of the lower classes was a use of their majority vote in the General Assembly. This could be used against the court in order to deprive it of its overgreat authority by transferring most of its functions to lesser lawcourts more in sympathy with the ordinary citizen.

The leader of this attack against the Areopagos was a popular political leader named Ephialtes, about whom little else is known than that (in Aristotle's words):

Being deemed incorruptible and loyal to the commonwealth, he attacked the Council and deprived it of all those prerogatives through which it had been guardian of the constitution, assigning some of these to the Senate of Five Hundred and others to the popular assembly and the other lawcourts.

But Ephialtes paid the penalty of his audacity. He was assassinated at night in a lightless street of the city, presumably with the connivance of Kimonian partisans in retaliation for their leader's banishment into exile.

For an unexpected train of circumstances had given Kimon's opponents a welcome opportunity to topple him from power. A previous attempt to do so had failed when, on his return to Athens from his conquest of the island of Thasos and summary acquisition of the gold mines on the opposite mainland, he was made to stand trial on the charge that he had not led his armies farther into Macedon because the Macedonian king had secretly bribed him to refrain from invading his country. On this occasion (according to Plutarch's somewhat contradictory account) Pericles was the most vehement in his accusation of Kimon, yet at the actual trial the mildest of his prosecutors. Perhaps Pericles realized that conviction was not possible on a charge incapable of proof. Not surprisingly, Kimon was acquitted. But far more serious trouble soon beset him.

A year before the trial an appalling earthquake destroyed Sparta, shaking down most of the houses and killing those of its younger boys who chanced to be in a gymnasium at the time. Martial law was proclaimed – a step made all the more necessary when the Helot serfs in the Lacedemonian countryside seized the opportunity to attempt a general insurrection. This was suppressed locally; but a more serious development evolved in neighbouring Messenia where the dissident inhabitants took refuge in the mountain stronghold of Ithome and resisted all Spartan attempts to dislodge them. After more than a year of futile effort Sparta turned to Athens for help. An acrimonious debate ensued in the Athenian assembly, in which Ephialtes of the people's party opposed lending any assistance to Athens' most formidable rival and potential enemy, while Kimon of the aristocratic faction, which had consistently maintained friendly relations with Sparta, pleaded that Greece could not afford to be politically disunited as long as Persia still posed a threat to its liberty. Preferring Sparta's survival to Athens' aggrandizement, Kimon persuaded the people to send a large force to Sparta's assistance for the capture of Ithome.

The outcome belied Kimon's expectations. During the still protracted siege, Spartan suspicions were somehow aroused against their Athenian helpers. Anticipating treachery, the Spartans abruptly dismissed their Athenian ally, whose humiliated and indignant soldiers returned home empty-handed: whereupon the Athenian people, enraged at this uncalled-for and offensive treatment, vented its displeasure on Kimon, whose pro-Spartan leanings had been directly responsible for the affair. By majority vote Kimon suffered ostracism for the usual ten-year term and in consequence was obliged to leave Athens.

Unexpected as this incident was, its sequel was even more surprising. Ill will between the two great military powers led to complete estrangement when shortly after the Messenian misunderstanding a Spartan expeditionary force was dispatched to Delphi to 'free' it from Phocian control, which Athens had supported. On their return from Delphi the Spartan forces encamped a short distance north of the Attic frontier, at Tanagra; and it was there the Athenians marched out to oppose them. Now it was open war between Athens and Sparta.

At this juncture Kimon, now in his fourth year of exile, gave proof of his unalterable devotion to the land that had cast him out. Inasmuch as the Athenian army had overstepped the frontier of Attica by advancing to Tanagra, Kimon could join it without fear of arrest. But when he offered to marshal the men of his tribe to fight against the Spartans, and word of this reached Athens, the assembly voted that he was to be debarred from the ranks on the ground that there was risk of treachery because of his well-known pro-Spartan proclivities.

According to Plutarch's vivid account:

[Kimon] thereupon left the army after exhorting those of his fellow countrymen most suspected of favouring the Spartan cause to comport themselves so courageously against the enemy that the falsity of the charge against them would be manifest to all. These, then, being a hundred in number, set up Kimon's armour in the midst of their company and fought around it against the foe with such desperation that every man of them was slain. In deep regret for the loss of such heroic fighters and repenting of their unjust suspicion of their loyalty, the Athenians did not long maintain their harshness against Kimon; but having been defeated in the great Tanagra battle and dreading lest the Spartans would invade their land in the coming spring, they recalled him from exile. . . . And Kimon, as soon as he returned, put an end to the war by reconciling the two powers.

During Kimon's brief absence in exile the ascendancy of the aristocratic party must have suffered a considerable setback, being deprived of its great leader and no longer drawing support from the Council of the Areopagos, which had by now been reduced to a lawcourt with jurisdiction over murder trials only (much as it appears in Aeschylus' *Eumenides*, produced in 458 B.C., quite possibly the very year in which Ephialtes was murdered). But Kimon's recall from exile and his ensuing arbitration of the conflict with Sparta more than restored him to popular favour, with consequent enhancement of his political authority.

Kimon was by this time a very rich man in his own right as well as by his intimate connexion with Athens' wealthiest citizen, Kallias, who had married his sister Elpinike. How Kimon acquired his fortune is not difficult to guess, since his position of supreme command in so many successful engagements, particularly in those against Persian forces, must have been highly lucrative to him personally. From his well-established affluence he proceeded to win political partisans to himself from among the poorer citizens by lavish gifts indiscriminately distributed. He sought further to increase his popularity by planting plane trees to shade the public gathering place of the Agora and laying out parks and playgrounds throughout the city, with especial attention to converting the Academy quarter from a 'bare, dry, and dirty tract to a well-watered grove with shady alleys to walk in and open courses for races'.

Against this farflung liberality, Pericles, in spite of substantial inherited wealth, could hardly hope to compete; but, once he was in power, there occurred to him a far more effective way of winning approval of the multitude – by distributing the wealth of the State in lieu of his own personal revenues. Since this action bears directly on the construction of the Parthenon, it merits more detailed exposition.

To Aristides is ascribed the original organization of the Delian League as a confederation of Greek states (mainly islanders) for offence and defence against Persian aggression. For building up the League's effective resources the members were allowed to contribute at their option either ships of war or a monetary equivalent. The assessments made by Aristides in this connexion were generally accepted as so equitable that they won him the nickname which, in the famous anecdote, moved one Athenian to vote for his ostracism out of sheer surfeit of hearing him called 'The Just'. The League's title was derived from the fact that the synod of its members conducted its affairs from the temple of Apollo and Artemis on the mid-Aegean island of Delos. There the monetary contributions of the League were deposited, with a board of treasurers (the *Hellenotamiai*) appointed to administer their use.

In the course of a few decades, as more and more of the members commuted their annual contributions from ships to money, till only three of the islands (Chios, Lesbos and Samos) still drew from their navies for the League's activities, the so-called Confederation became an adjunct of Athens' own political policies, with Athens building and equipping the ships and training and paying the crews with the funds supplied by the other members. In this manner the first Athenian Empire was evolved, largely under Kimon's initiative.

Meanwhile the funds of the League continued to be deposited in the temple at Delos, whence conceivably some dissident member seceding from the League might appropriate them to its own use. It was a natural – and perhaps inevitable – precaution to transfer these funds, in which Athens had so large an interest, from tiny seagirt Delos to the mainland capital city. Accordingly in 454 B.C., at the proposal (it is said) of politically unstable Samos, the accumulated monetary capital of the League was removed to Athens, where the board of the *Helleno-tamiai* continued to administer it to Athens' best advantage.

It is very generally stated that Pericles was responsible for this trans-ference of the imperial treasury to his more immediate personal super-vision. But if the account offered in these pages is correct and Kimon was recalled from exile early in 456 B.C., to become once more his party's head and the State's political leader, then the transfer of the League treasury from Delos to Athens in 454 must have taken place under his aegis and not by Pericles' authority.

However there is nothing to show or even to suggest that Kimon made any use of the League funds, now so accessible to him, for any other than its original and proper purpose of equipping and maintain-ing the ostensibly confederate, but in fact little else than Athenian, navy. Indeed, if we may trust the accuracy of Plutarch's report that Pericles' diversion of the League's treasury for the beautification of Athens with new and costly buildings 'was the one of all his actions which his enemies eyed most askance and cried out against in the popu-lar assemblies', we can hardly suppose that the Kimonian opposition would have taxed Pericles with this misuse of funds, if Kimon himself had already practised it.

On the contrary, if Kimon drew on the League's treasury it would have been entirely in accord with the League's established aim to re-strain the advance of Persian power. For in the fourth year after the transference of the League treasury to Athens, Kimon embarked on an ambitious enterprise to break the Persian hold on Egypt and Cyprus and thereby roll back the western fringe of the Great King's enormous empire. The effort failed and the two-pronged expedition was given up when – whether through wound in battle or illness from disease – Kimon died on the island of Cyprus and the fleet returned to Athens with the corpse of its illustrious commander.

'From this time forward', wrote George Grote in his eminently readable and still serviceable *History of Greece*, 'no further operations were undertaken by Athens and her confederacy against the Persians.' And it appears that 'a convention was concluded' between Athens and the Great King. This was the famous Peace of Kallias, about which modern historians have long held dispute. But if indeed there was such a treaty concluded at Kimon's death, then the fact that it was Kimon's brother-in-law who negotiated it makes it one of the great achievements of the Kimonian party, now heading for two decades of decline. For Kimon's death marked the collapse of the aristocratic faction in politics.

On Ephialtes' assassination during Kimon's absence in exile, the leadership of the popular party devolved on Pericles, at that time only in his thirty-second year. Previous to this accession to power he seems to have taken no very active part in public life, being (it is only just to say) a renegade to his class and proper party and on that account not readily winning the common people's trust and favour. Of aristocratic lineage (being, in Plutarch's phrase, 'of noblest birth both on his father's and mother's side'), he allied himself with the common people through political expediency 'to gain a foothold for himself and find means to work against Kimon'. For there was long-standing enmity between the two families. Pericles' father, Xanthippos, had precipitated the disgrace and the ruinous fine inflicted on Kimon's father, Miltiades; and later, in 462, Pericles had brought public accusation against Kimon, seeking to have him fined, like his father, for abuse of his military command. Perhaps we should not believe Plutarch's tale that, after Kimon's death, Pericles sent out one of Kimon's sons with a pitifully inadequate flotilla in the expectation of discrediting him by making him seem to side with the Spartans whom he could not hope to defeat. Yet there is presumably truth in Plutarch's further charge that Pericles 'made it somewhat his business to prevent Kimon's sons from rising in the service of the state'.

A more firmly attested and even more striking instance of Pericles' inveterate and unscrupulous political activity against his lifelong adversary occurred in 450 B.C. while Kimon was still alive. It will be recalled that in the spring of that year Kimon was in command of the Athenian allied forces in an expedition against the island of Cyprus. During his absence from his native land of Attica Pericles introduced into the popular assembly, and succeeded in getting ratified, a decree to the effect that only those whose father and mother were both native-born Athenians could continue to be enrolled as citizens. Whatever its ostensible purpose, its immediate intent would have been to divest Kimon of Athenian citizenship and therewith of his military command and political power, inasmuch as his mother Hegesipyle was a Thracian princess and not herself a citizen of Athens.

The sudden death of Kimon in Cyprus, before the provisions of the new law could be exercised against him, presumably explains why this law was not enforced in Athens at the time of its passage, but remained in abeyance until, several years later, a new element of popular self-interest was introduced by the arrival of a munificent gift of a shipment of grain from Egypt to be distributed among all Athenian citizens. The failure to implement the law at the time it was originally decreed shows that it was little else than an underhanded political move by Pericles against his illustrious political opponent. The countering decree providing for the construction of a Temple to Victory overlooking the ascent to the Acropolis may well have been the reply of the Kimonian party to Pericles' outrageous assault on their leader.

Of course, it may very well be that Pericles championed the Athenian lower classes through genuine interest in their welfare and sincere attachment to their cause, and not solely for considerations of political expediency and personal dislike for Kimon. Yet he never became – or gave any sign of seeking to become – one with the people in thought or act, but held himself apart from them with a mien so condescendingly superior that he would have alienated their affection, were it not that (paradoxically) they admired and excused his Olympian aloofness for the sake of the intellectual prestige and protection that it conferred. Certainly, however much it may have contributed to his own political supremacy, the intensity of his patriotism was beyond dispute with its whole-hearted desire to make Athens splendidly great. More intelligent than Kimon and with a breadth of social vision denied to the conservative aristocrats, the ambitious mind of Pericles, more than any other single factor, created the artistic and political greatness of fifth-century Athens. The two decades of his absolute control of the Attic commonwealth – from Kimon's death in 450 to his own demise during the plague in 429 – have rightly taken their title of the Periclean Age from this remarkable man.

Nevertheless he seems to have been scrupulously unfair towards his political adversaries; and his raid on the national wealth, including the sums contributed by Athens' allies for their mutual defence, however stimulating to the local economy, was hardly of lasting benefit to the general prosperity. But the immediate results were highly gratifying – especially to the beneficiaries of governmental largesse.

A series of monetary reforms – some of which had perhaps been conceived by Ephialtes – was shrewdly contrived to better the financial condition of the poorer classes and confirm their party loyalty. A fixed rate of pay for the jurors was established for the lawcourts (whereas *dikasts* had previously been obliged to serve gratuitously). Troops under arms, hitherto drawing only 'maintenance money', now earned regular pay, as did the oarsmen and others of the crews in training for the fleet. There was even a fund for defraying the entrance fee to the dramatic festivals in the theatre of Dionysos for those who could not afford the admission. The threat of an idle surplus populace was dispelled by sending out colonists to settle foreign lands that for one reason or another could not oppose their coming. Finally, those that remained at home were assured employment from an ambitious programme of public works, for which the price of materials and the charge for labour were to be met by the state treasury.

Heading the list of these enterprises of economic incentive to every craftsman and artisan and unskilled workman was the remodelled and immensely costly Parthenon, to be followed, on its completion, by a monumental marble gateway to the Acropolis – the far-famed Propylaea.

In his *Constitution of the Athenians* Aristotle remarks:

And so it came to pass that more than 20,000 men were supported from the revenues and taxes. There were 6,000 dikasts; 1,600 archers and 1,200 horsemen; a Council of 500; for the arsenal, 500 guards and 50 more for the Acropolis; 700 local magistrates, and 700 foreign ones; later on, in wartime, 2,500 heavy-armed soldiers, 20 guardships and other craft, transporting 2,000 men chosen by lot for guard duty and revenue service; and in addition to all these, the occupants of the prytaneion, the orphans, the prison officials. This entire number drew their maintenance from the public funds.

As for the public construction works, chief among which was the Parthenon with its ivory-plated and gold-coated colossal cult statue of Athena, there is an often quoted passage in Plutarch's *Life of Pericles* which catalogues the vast amount of material and the enormous number of craftsmen and artisans engaged upon the project, to this effect:

The materials to be employed were marble, bronze, ivory, gold, ebony, and cypress wood; while the craftsmen to work and utilize these were carpenters, moulders, bronze-casters, masons, dyers, goldsmiths and workers of ivory, painters, broiderers, embossers, not to mention the furnishers and transporters of the materials, among which were dealers and sailors and steersmen by sea and wheelwrights and waggoners and breeders of yoke animals by land. Also there were rope-makers, weavers, leather-workers, road-builders, and miners. And since each craft and occupation had its own company of slave and free under its orders, one might say that every age and every capacity were marshalled into service.

So the complex task progressed until, after nine years, the 40-foot gold-and-ivory cult statue was installed in Athena's new sanctuary under supervision of its designer, the sculptor Pheidias; while the great temple that enclosed it now stood complete, as its master-builder Iktinos had designed it, with its coloured mouldings and coffered ceilings of wood within and marble without, its tall and ornate folding doors and gilded bronze grilles. Only the sculpture for its two pediments, and perhaps some carving on its 225-foot-long wallcrown frieze, were still to be added.

And in all this stirring enterprise, made possible by lavish dispensation of imperial wealth, the architect who had been in charge of the older and slower-building temple of less ambitious plan, whom we have identified as Kallikrates, had (as we shall see) no part or portion except in so far as he was accorded the unexciting task of erecting high blank walls between the city and the sea, to unite Athens securely with its harbour of Peiraeus.

3: Kallikrates

A fragmentary inscription in letters of the middle years of the fifth century B.C. (now in the Epigraphical Museum, Athens) preserves part of a decree commissioning Kallikrates to make some sort of construction to prevent vagabond slaves and thieves from gaining entrance to the Acropolis. It does not follow from this scrap of information that when the high south wall of the Acropolis was built with money supplied by Kimon from the spoils of the Eurymedon battle (as Plutarch relates) it was to Kallikrates that Kimon entrusted the task of constructing these defences; but such an inference is at least permissible. It is rendered somewhat more probable by the entry in the Parthenon building accounts for the year 443–442 B.C. naming Kallikrates in connexion with one of the Long Walls to the sea, since we read in the same passage of Plutarch that the foundations of the Long Walls were likewise laid by Kimon from the Eurymedon spoils. To be sure, the last of the three long walls (to which the Parthenon accounts must refer) was constructed under the aegis of Pericles; and Pericles was (as we have seen) no friend of Kimon or Kallikrates. Indeed, if we lend credence to the gibe of the contemporary comic poet Kratinos as quoted by Plutarch to the effect that

> 'Tis long since Pericles, if words could do it,
> Talks the wall up; yet adds not one whit to it!

it would appear that, far from facilitating Kallikrates' assignment, Pericles did his utmost to obstruct it.

We have therefore reasonably good ground for taking Kallikrates as Kimon's supervising architect for his building projects.

This presumption is greatly strengthened by a second marble slab found in 1897 on the north slope of the Acropolis. This too is inscribed in letters of the mid fifth century, and records a decree of the Athenian

29. Athena Nike temple

popular assembly 'to appoint a priestess of Athena Nike with life tenure, and to provide her sanctuary with a doorway in accord with Kallikrates' specifications. . . . And to cause a temple to be built in accord with Kallikrates' specifications, and a marble altar'. Not all of this part of the decree is fully legible; and its concluding portion is lost.

Various matters connected with this document have been subject to discussion in recent years; but it is generally agreed that it concerns construction of a temple for Athena Nike on the site of the extant small temple on the bastion overlooking the ascent to the Acropolis; that it probably dates from the year 450–449 or 449–448 B.C.; and that – contrary to its specific provisions – *no temple was built at that time in that location*. Instead, it has been established on unobjectionable evidence that the surviving temple to Athena Nike [29] was erected during the early years of the Peloponnesian war with Sparta, most probably in 427–426 B.C. and hence more than twenty years after the original promulgation of the decree and a couple of years after Pericles' death from the plague in 429. It may be taken as significant that the years during which the construction of the temple was delayed coincide almost exactly with the period of Pericles' political control of the Athenian state.

In view of the date of the sanctioning decree, it has been very generally presumed that the temple to 'Athena Victory' was intended to commemorate the treaty of peace with Persia negotiated by Kimon's brother-in-law Kallias shortly after Kimon's sudden death in 450 B.C. But no reason is suggested for the suspension of the decree's seemingly mandatory provision 'to cause a temple to be built in accord with Kallikrates' specifications' – an act that is always considered a complete mystery. Yet surely there is no mystery here at all!

If the miniature temple was voted in recognition of Kimon's military achievements and Kallias' diplomatic success, as the date of the decree pointedly suggests, it would have become an enduring memorial to Pericles' lifelong political enemy, of a kind that Pericles would not have tolerated with equanimity. Consequently, when he came into power at Kimon's death he cancelled its construction, in much the same manner as he arrested Kimon's great project of Athena's temple on the hilltop of the Acropolis, to replace it with a more splendid design under supervision of a new master-builder of Pericles' own choosing, Iktinos.

But when Pericles unexpectedly was removed by death and the Kimonian party under new leadership resumed control, one of its first acts was to resurrect the discarded project of a temple to Victory-in-

Battle (for such was the role of the goddess Nike) to honour the memory of their great general and party leader Kimon – the marble chapel whose construction Pericles had prevented.

There is an unexpected corollary to this unedifying incident of political obstruction and party enmity; for, actually, Kallikrates managed to build the temple of his designing, and at very nearly the time of the decree, but it did not stand on the bastion of the Acropolis

30. Ilissos temple, engraving, Stuart and Revett, 1762

and it was not dedicated to the city's patron goddess, Victorious Athena. The facts are these:

There was a temple on the banks of the Ilissos not far from the place where – according to Plato – Socrates and the fair young Phaidros once sat discoursing on love and rhetoric. It was later incorporated in a Christian church and finally pulled down in the late 1770s, but not before it had been recorded by Stuart and Revett [30]. Their careful

31. Athena Nike temple, engraving, C. Hansen, 1839

drawings reveal its extraordinarily close resemblance, in plan, proportion and detail, to the temple of Athena Nike which was eventually built beside the entrance to the Acropolis [31]. Most recent authorities have therefore attributed the Ilissos temple to Kallikrates.

If the plans of the two buildings are set side by side as in [32], this mutual resemblance is instantly evident. In the two elevations [30 and 31], also, no differences are discernible by the unaided eye, except for a slight change of scale and the presence of the canonic three-banded Ionic epistyle on the Nike temple as opposed to the blank one on the Ilissos temple. (The frieze carvings of the Ilissos temple had been removed before Stuart and Revett reached Athens [34 and 35].) In the two ground plans the only striking difference is the addition of an entry room behind the front columns of the Ilissos temple – or perhaps we should say the omission of such a room from the Nike temple. Apart from these discrepancies (for which a ready explanation will present itself), while there is a difference in absolute size amounting to about 9 per cent in favour of the Ilissos temple, the mutual *proportions* of the various constituent elements of the two buildings are virtually identical. Indeed, if the entry room were omitted from the Ilissos temple and all its remaining parts were reduced by three thirty-seconds* of their size, the Ilissos temple would become the Nike temple . . . except for one highly peculiar feature. Whereas the columns of the two temples show the anticipated difference of $\frac{3}{32}$ in their height, the elements supported by the columns (the entablature of the Order) have not been reduced comparably, but are within an inch of identical size.

I characterize this as a highly peculiar feature because one of the fundamental tenets of classical Greek architecture (it is always sup-

---

* $\frac{3}{32}$ may seem an improbable arithmetical factor to have been employed, until it is recalled that the ancient Greek foot was subdivided into 16 'fingers' instead of our duodecimal inches; so that this particular fraction represents a diminution by exactly $1\frac{1}{2}$ fingers in every foot.

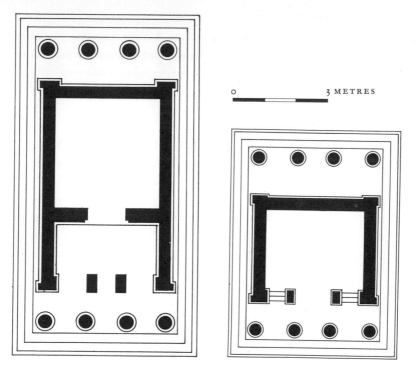

32. Ilissos temple (*left*) and Athena Nike temple (*right*), ground plans

posed) is strict adherence to an established harmony of proportions in every part; and that tenet is here visibly, even conspicuously, disregarded. For, if the Order of either of these temples was correctly proportioned according to contemporary architectural taste, then the Order of the other temple could not have been so – unless, of course, taste had changed during the intervening period between their construction. But it can be shown that aesthetic preference moved quite consistently towards a lighter entablature; so that the Nike temple, being, despite its proportionately heavier entablature, the later building (as will presently be proved), violates this rule.

But before examining the relative chronology of the two temples it is pertinent to point out the unusual features that ally them intimately to each other and at the same time set them apart from the general norm. In the first place, Greek temples ordinarily, in consequence of their pronounced rectangular shape, have for their interior sanctuary a room considerably longer than wide. But in these two temples the interior room is an almost exact square.

Secondly, although a colonnaded vestibule at the eastern entrance end of a temple is usually (but not invariably) balanced by a corresponding one at the rear, this feature has been omitted in both our temples.

Thirdly and much more abnormally, rectangular piers (preserved in Nike and well assured for Ilissos) have been substituted for the round columns traditionally used between, or in front of, the wall ends (in architectural terms, antae). It is difficult to divine the reason for this departure from an almost universal tradition, unless it was the thought that supports in this shape harmonized with the pier-like wall ends between which they stood and with which they co-operated in carrying the ceiling of the vestibule, better than round columns responding to the exterior colonnade, with which they had no functional connexion.

Finally, a very special interest and importance attach to the moulded circular bases of the Ionic columns at front and rear; for in these, when taken in conjunction with the wallbase moulding of the Kimonian Parthenon, the individual creative talent of Kallikrates is manifested.

These mouldings mark an important stage in the development of the Ionic column base used in Asia Minor – where the Ionic order originated – to the harmoniously proportioned 'classic' Attic base. The profile of this classic base, as seen in the Propylaea and Erechtheion, is so close to that devised by Kallikrates for the Ilissos and Nike temples [33] that we may justly claim for him a crucial role in creating a prototype that was to pass into the vocabulary of classical architecture and to be revived in the Renaissance.

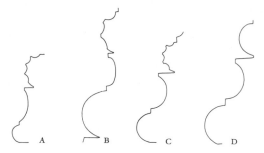

33. Column bases: (A) Athena Nike, (B) Propylaea,
(C) Erechtheion, east porch, (D) Erechtheion, north porch

To revert to the intimately related temples of Athena Nike and the unknown deity housed on the slope of the Ilissos, there can be no difference of opinion as to which of the two buildings was the elder, inasmuch as the dates of their construction can be fixed within narrow limits. As we know, the provisions of the decree of about the year 450–449 B.C. authorizing a temple for Athena Nike were not carried out until 427–426. On the other hand the Ilissos temple must have been built very soon after the decree for the Nike temple was ignored or countermanded. The evidence on this head is twofold.

Firstly, imported Parian island marble was employed for the figured frieze of the temple, while the remainder of the structure consisted of marble from the local Attic quarries of Mt Pentelikon. The significance of this observation lies in the fact that, whereas Parian marble, being of finer grain and better quality, had been favoured by earlier Attic builders for the sculptured adjuncts to their temples and was so used on the Hephaisteion (begun in 447–446), the Periclean Parthenon broke with this tradition by employing Pentelic marble, despite its comparatively coarser grain and occasional streaks of mica, for its carved wall-crown frieze (the famous 'Panathenaic' frieze of the Elgin marbles) and the statuary for its two pediments. This is a reasonably reliable indication that the Ilissos temple preceded the initiation of· these

34. Ilissos temple, detail of frieze

portions of the Periclean Parthenon and therefore could not have been built much later than 440 B.C.

Secondly, more precise chronological evidence derives from the sculptural style of the exterior frieze of the Order on the Ilissos temple [34

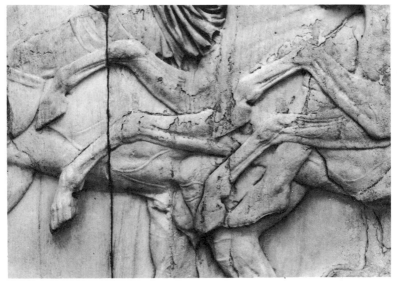

36. Parthenon, detail of frieze

35. Ilissos temple, detail of frieze

and 35]. To the trained eye it is immediately clear that these reliefs must have been carved at least a decade earlier than the wall frieze of the Parthenon [36, 37] and that by comparing them with other surviving Attic sculpture they belong stylistically to the early 440s.

37. Parthenon, detail of frieze

Taking this in conjunction with the well attested acrimonious hostility between the two leading political parties in the Athenian state, the course of events pertaining to the temples and their architect becomes clear. After Kimon's death and on Pericles' succession to political control, Kallikrates was removed from his position as architect in charge of construction on the Acropolis, yet managed nonetheless – through party support? or with funds supplied by Kallias or Kimon's heirs? – to carry out his plans for the temple to Nike by building it in honour of some other deity, not on the lofty bastion overlooking the ascent to the Acropolis, but in an inconspicuous site low down beyond the city wall.

If this conclusion is sound, it follows that the uninformative phrase of the original decree, 'to cause a temple to be built in accord with Kallikrates' specifications', finds its full elucidation in the Ilissos temple; for from examination of this latter building we can recover Kallikrates' original plan as he intended it for Athena Nike on the Acropolis.

Yet, if this is so, an obvious objection will have to be overcome, since it must occur to everyone to demand why, then, were not the two temples completely and precisely identical instead of showing certain differences in their plans? (It will be recalled that the Nike temple is not only somewhat smaller, but also lacks the entry room of its counterpart.)

The effective reply to this query is simple and has often been given: at the time when the Nike temple was finally built in 427–426 B.C., Pericles' monumental new gateway to the Acropolis, the present Propylaea, was already in place; and its south-west wing, while not as extensive as had been planned, nevertheless left no room for a full-size replica of the Ilissos temple on its intended site. The plan reproduced in [38] will make the situation clear.

A south-west wing for the Propylaea to correspond precisely to the completed north-west wing opposite had certainly been projected, but with even greater certainty the plan had never been carried out. Ob-

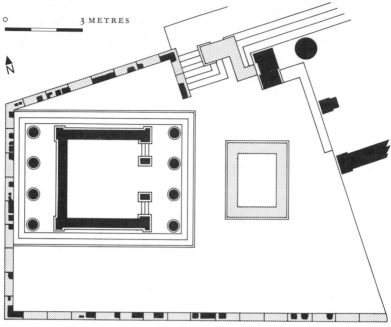

N

38. Bastion, Athena Nike temple and altar, ground plan

struction to its completion in the intended size had arisen, perhaps because of the circuit wall of the Acropolis, which ran across a corner of the terrain, or perhaps because the area behind the wall was sacred to Artemis and therefore inviolate. Whatever the determining reason, a sharply curtailed version was substituted for the larger structure demanded by strict axial symmetry of plan. It is true that there was still left free space enough for reproducing the Ilissos temple at full size on the bastion. But then there would have been no place for an altar in front of the temple and no free area for the requisite ritual ceremonies. For this reason a shorter (but not necessarily narrower) structure had to be devised. This was accomplished by omitting the entry room to the inner chamber; and in order to keep this abbreviated version in correct overall proportion the scale of the building was diminished throughout (except for the entablature over the columns). Further, a different treatment and new subject matter were chosen for the sculptured frieze, more in accord with contemporary taste and style.

In all other respects the congruence of the two temples is so pronounced and so visibly evident as to admit no doubt that one and the same architect was responsible for both. The evidence is equally emphatic that this architect was Kallikrates.

Shortly after Pericles' death and at about the same time that the Nike temple was being built, the Athenians undertook construction of a temple to Apollo on that god's sacred mid-Aegean island of Delos [39].

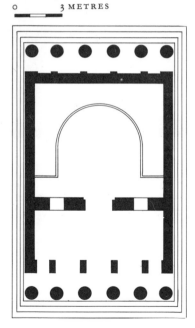

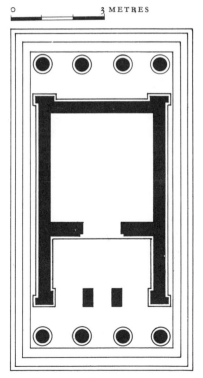

39. Temple of the Athenians, Delos, ground plan
drawn to half scale of [40]

40. Ilissos temple ground plan

Its plan resembles Kallikrates' Ilissos temple [40] in so many respects that recent scholarly opinion has more and more inclined to view it as the work of the same architect, more especially because it contains several features unparalleled in fifth-century architecture except in work attributable to this master.

In fact, so intimately are the two plans related, that if six columns in place of four were set at front and rear of the Ilissos temple, with a corresponding row of four instead of two rectangular piers for the vestibule, the ground plan of the Delos temple would automatically be produced except for a few very minor differences. The only novel features at Delos are the addition of a fourth step to the temple platform, the introduction of a series of shallow attached pilasters to the exterior of the rear wall in repetition of the pilasters at the wall ends, and the insertion of windows between the entry room and the sanctuary for more light and to give visitors the opportunity of viewing the contents of this sanctuary without passing the barrier of its grilled doorway. The hemicycle in this interior room outlines a pedestal on which were displayed seven more-than-lifesize statues moved from a nearby building – which presumably supplies the reason for the windows in the partition wall.

As against these slight differences the correspondence between the two ground plans is almost spectacular. In both are to be seen freestanding columns at front and rear with no exterior colonnade and no rear vestibule room; treatment of the front vestibule as a separate unit of unusual depth, with rectangular piers instead of the normal round columns; and a reduction of the long rectangle usually assigned to the sanctuary of a temple, so that the interior chamber has become very nearly square. It cannot be claimed for this last feature that its abnormal shape was forced on the architect by the exigencies of the available area (as may well have been the case for the Nike temple and, by transference, the temple on the Ilissos), but must reflect the architect's own deliberate preference.

Nevertheless, although the two ground plans are so very much alike, no comparisons can be drawn between the structures themselves; for whereas the Nike and Ilissos temples were of the Ionic Order, the temple on Delos was designed in the Doric style; and the two structural systems are so distinct in every part that comparable details scarcely exist.

However, there is a point of contact with another Doric temple of Attic workmanship and of nearly contemporary date. This is the temple of Hephaistos topping the rise of ground above the ancient judicial and administrative centre of Athens, the Agora. Long known to the modern world as the Theseion – and still so called by tourists and native

41. Hephaisteion (Theseion), west façade

Athenians – the correct name of the temple has in recent years been restored to it by archaeologists. If its remarkably well-preserved façade [41] is confronted with that of the Delian temple as restored by F. Courby [42] even the most experienced eye will be unable to detect any greater likeness than might have been found in any other pair of Doric hexastyle temples of fifth-century origin.

There are the same supporting steps to the platform (except that the Delos temple shows four instead of three), the same channelled columns with squat cylindrical capital and square abacus block, and for superstructure above the columns the same sequence of blank epistyle (or architrave) surmounted by a frieze of alternating triglyphs and metopes

42. Temple of the Athenians, Delos, engraving by F. Courby

and, above these, the same horizontal and low-pitched sloping cornice with upturned gutter defining the angle of the roof and, together with the horizontal cornice, framing the sharply acute triangle of the pediment. Nor are the proportions of the various parts to one another noticeably different. The columns of the Hephaisteion seem to be set slightly wider apart and its epistyle looks a trifle heavier in relation to the frieze that it carries; but otherwise it would be difficult to point to any specific dissimilarity between the two temple fronts. And yet . . .

It is common knowledge that the distinctive elements of the Greek Orders were repeated from the fifth century into Hellenistic times with no appreciable alteration of their characteristic shapes and patterns. The architects' activities were not directed towards expressing their individual talent by inventing hitherto unfamiliar structural elements with which to create an original style of wholly new appearance. Instead, they accepted without challenge the shapes and patterns traditional to the Orders and devoted themselves to adapting their size or their outline to suit a changing artistic taste, as when they diminished the pronounced parabolic curve of the Doric capital or modified to a hardly appreciable degree the convolutions of its Ionic counterpart. Or again, they slightly altered the proportionate size of some element of an Order, to embody some specific numerical harmony in the measurements that they assigned to its visibly distinct component parts (for an example, consider the accompanying diagram of an Ionic order [43]).

If the measured harmonies of this 'music made visible' were to be apprehended by the beholder, it was essential that its separate notes or tones – by which I mean metaphorically the individual elements of the Order – should not be blurred or mingled or otherwise confused with one another, but should reach the beholder with absolute distinctness and clarity. To this end in all three of the Orders care was taken to set off, and even keep organically apart, the various structural elements by bordering them with a brilliantly coloured band, on which were carved or painted certain traditional decorative patterns. By such bands of

43. Temple of Athena Polias, Priene, Ionic Order

The ancient foot was divided into 4 palms and the palm into 4 fingers.
The length of foot varied locally;
at Priene the foot equals approximately 11½″.

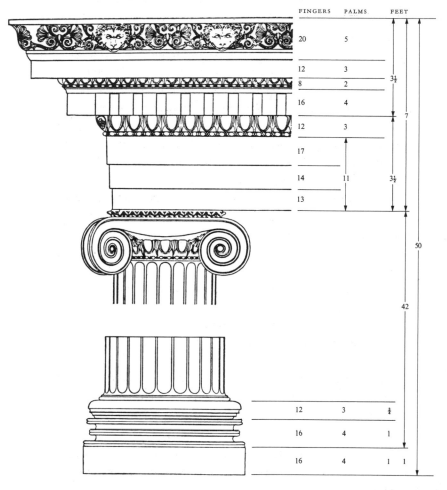

coloured ornament I am referring to the architectural mouldings that today, with their bright colours lost, are little seen or long remembered by any but the most informed of modern visitors to the ancient sites.

And yet these carved and coloured (or on occasion merely painted) 'string courses' – to borrow a term from the vocabulary of later masonry – served the ancient Greek architects as a visual language, whose idiom was thoroughly understood by them and may well have been understood by their public. We are fortunate in having all the surviving examples of these classical string course mouldings accessible in full size linear renderings of their sectional contours (or 'profiles', as they are known technically). These profiles were recorded with the aid of an adjustable template which could be fitted exactly to all the ins-and-outs of projection and recession of a carved surface. Copied directly from the template's record, the *Profiles of Greek Mouldings* (to give them the title under which they were published in two folio volumes*) were sorted into types, arranged in chronological order, and accompanied with a commentary by the indefatigable author, who tracked them down through mainland, island, and Asia Minor Greek sites and transferred their images to sheets of paper from which they finally reappeared at their full natural size in her monumental monograph – a *monumentum* not only *aere* but perhaps even *marmore perennius*.

There are, then, two sorts of criteria, one dependent on proportions, the other on profiles of mouldings, which may be applied to the surviving specimens of Greek classic architecture with some chance of discovering the individual identity of their designers. (*See* Note 5 on page 170.)

And in view of the accumulated evidence set out in Note 5 it may fairly be asserted that a close-knit chain of coincidences connects the Nike temple to the temple on the Ilissos, this latter to the Athenian

---

* By Dr Lucy T. Shoe, Harvard University Press, 1936. Supplemented by *Profiles of Western Greek Mouldings*, American Academy in Rome, 1952.

temple on Delos, and from this by way of identical proportions leads to the temple of Ares in Athens (as recovered by Professor Dinsmoor) and by way of identical mouldings to the Hephaisteion [44], and so finally extends to the entire group of Doric temples, including the temple of Poseidon at Sunion [45] and the never completed temple of Nemesis at Rhamnus, attributed by Professor Dinsmoor to the same 'nameless architect'. Further we are led back from the Hephaisteion to the Kimonian Parthenon by two peculiarly individual mannerisms, to wit, the substitution of limestone for marble in the bottom step of the temple and the (illogical) introduction of an *Ionic* moulded wall and anta-base into a Doric structure – a trait rejected by the Periclean architects but used once more, in modified but basically identical profile, in the temple of Poseidon at Sunion.

That the architect responsible for this impressive series of temples was Kallikrates is shown by the chance survival of the Athenian decree empowering Kallikrates to construct a temple for Athena Nike and by Plutarch's mention of Kallikrates and Iktinos as the architects of the Parthenon. (A notice that I have interpreted to mean that Kallikrates was the architect of the Parthenon which was subsequently embodied in the enlarged Periclean temple. Perhaps it deserves more than passing comment that if Kallikrates had been no more than Iktinos' assistant or foreman he would hardly have been named ahead of him by Plutarch.)

If the objection is raised that so prolific and important an artist in the golden age of Attic architecture would surely have been named more frequently in ancient literature, it should be replied that a like silence enshrouds the names of most of the architects who built the temples, public colonnades, and monumental gateways in Greek lands. It is true that we are familiar with the names of several of the architects of the great Ionic temples of Asia Minor. But there are no names on record for any of the builders of the Doric temples of Sicily and Southern Italy. More remarkably, we nowhere read the name of the master of his craft who designed the Erechtheion for the Acropolis of Athens, the most

44. Hephaisteion (Theseion), south-west corner and west end of south colonnade

45. Temple of Poseidon, Sunion

exquisitely refined of all surviving ancient buildings! In itself the fact that Dinsmoor could speak of a 'nameless architect' for *four* temples from Periclean times should invalidate the objection that if Kallikrates designed any of them we must somehow have learned of it from the ancient writers.

After all, something is known about Kallikrates. From the inscription commissioning him to build a temple for Athena Nike we conclude that he was alive and active in 450–449 B.C. From the Parthenon building accounts we learn that in 443 he completed the middle (and last) of the three Long Walls between the city and the sea. Earlier than that, if we are convinced that he was master-builder for the Kimonian Parthenon, we must conclude that he was already prominent in his profession by about 465 B.C. And at the other end of his career, if he designed the temple of the Athenians for Delos, he must have still been able and active in the 420s. In that case he could have personally supervised the long-delayed Nike temple in 427–426. Leaving aside the difficult question of whether he may have had a part in designing the Erechtheion, we shall have to attribute to him a lifetime of at least seventy years, since on the strength of the evidence here adduced he could hardly have been born later than 495 B.C. and was still active about the year 425.

Availing ourselves of Dinsmoor's suggested dates for the four temples attributed by him to his 'nameless architect', we may schedule Kallikrates' professional career approximately as follows:

	At work on
c. 465–449 B.C.	Kimonian Parthenon
c. 449–448	Ionic Temple on the Ilissos
c. 448–442	Hephaisteion
c. 442–438	Temple of Poseidon at Sunion
c. 438–434	Temple of Ares in Acharnai
c. 434–432	Temple of Nemesis at Rhamnus
c. 427–426	Temple of Athena Nike
c. 426–421(?)	Temple of the Athenians on Delos

So impressive a list, covering so many years of continuous activity, argues a figure of very considerable importance for the history of Greek architecture. But if we ask ourselves the very natural question, was this prolific builder really a great architect? we may not find it easy to discover a satisfactory answer.

To begin with, we must take into account that the functions of the classic Greek architect differed greatly from those of his modern counterpart. It is of course true that our English term is derived directly from the Greek; but in the parent language *architektōn* literally signifies no more than 'builder-in-chief' or the French *chef d'atelier*. In view of the fact that the normal plan for a fifth-century temple was dictated by established tradition and the architect was free to realize this plan only in terms of one of the two accepted columnar styles, the Doric and the Ionic (to which a Corinthian variant of Ionic was added later), it was not his province to devise a novel plan or invent new schemes of construction and decoration. Rather than that, it was his appointed role to supply his corps of skilled workmen (who first and foremost were expert marble-cutters) with schedules of measurements and, on occasion, with full-size carved patterns to be duplicated over and over until they had amassed the store of identically shaped blocks in the required quantity. Thereafter it was his task to supervise the hoisting into place and the precise fitting and the firm fastening of all these blocks in the correct arrangement of the Order. Quite literally, and with all the implications adhering to the term, the Greek *architektōn* was the Master Builder. What, then, of Kallikrates?

Naturally we have no immediate way of knowing how capably he supervised his groups of marble-cutters and masons and metalworkers in shaping and fitting and pegging fast with iron clamps and dowels the marble blocks with which his buildings were put together. But judging from what can still be seen of his work, he attended to these more mechanical aspects of his profession with authority and skill. The fact that Kimon, and after him the surviving Kimonian party politic, commissioned him with the most important architectural projects in their control argues for his ability and competence.

Over and above this routine role of supervising builder, when plans were to be thought out and detail specifications prescribed, Kallikrates showed inventiveness of imagination and freedom from tradition in his Ilissos-Nike design and his temple on Delos. In the latter his use of attached pilasters to articulate an otherwise empty wall may have been his own idea. If so, he was the originator of a device on which subsequent architects through the centuries were to rely for manipulating chiaroscuro for tridimensional effect. And if, as previously suggested, he gave the impetus that moved the Ionic column base towards its superbly contoured classic form, he exerted an influence of major import on the art of architecture.

On the opposite page of the balance sheet of his attainments, his sense of overall proportion has been impugned in modern times because of a widely entertained unfavourable comparison of the Hephaisteion with the Periclean masterpieces of the Parthenon and Propylaea. Even after due allowance has been made for the vastly superior setting of Athena's temple on its hilltop against a sunny clear sky, and for the impression produced on us by the mere bulk of greater physical size, and lastly (and more subtly) by the colour contrast – whose cause I am completely at a loss to explain – between the golden tone that Pentelic marble has assumed under sunlight, wind, and rain on the loftier Acropolis and the lifeless greyish tint that these same atmospheric forces have imparted to the same material on the low-lying Kerameikos hill above the Agora – after allowance for all these disadvantageous factors for the Hephaisteion in inevitable contrast with the Parthenon, I think that it remains true that a feeling of ponderous inelasticity, an almost sullen mood of unresponsive stolidity, somehow emanates from the temple of Hephaistos.

And if such an indictment is correctly made, then Kallikrates cannot be rated the equal of Iktinos with his Parthenon or Mnesikles with his no less marvellous Propylaea. Unless there is a generous measure of self-deception in our buoyant response to our first glimpse of the Parthenon, a response to which we may have been conditioned by life-long expectation, Iktinos must have had knowledge of some half-hidden and half-revealed architectural formula that Kallikrates had failed to acquire. But in what (we well may demand) did this secret power lie?

It is time to turn to the Parthenon's second builder, the remarkable architect who devised and completed the second Parthenon.

4: Iktinos

For lack of specific written evidence we shall never know what all the motives were that prompted Pericles to dismiss Kallikrates from his post of master-builder for the Parthenon. The decision to build a larger and finer shrine for the city's guardian goddess may have been a primary source of discord between the new all-powerful statesman and the supervising architect who could hardly have been willing to agree to undo so much of his work of more than a dozen years. But the suspension of 'Victorious Athena's' other temple also, despite the formal decree for its erection, suggests that political antagonism rather than personal animosity was responsible for the replacement of Kallikrates by Iktinos as part of a Periclean veto on all 'Kimonian' activities on the Acropolis. Henceforth we find Kallikrates engaged only on lesser projects within and especially beyond the city limits. His most important undertaking, begun immediately after the loss of his Parthenon commission as though in compensation for it, the temple of Hephaistos overlooking the meeting-place of the Agora, also seems to have been held in abeyance when only three-quarters completed.

As for the drastic change of plan for the Parthenon, Pericles and his artistic advisers (among whom Pheidias is reported to have ranked first) may have condemned the previous shape as outmoded with its length overgreat for its breadth. Then again, Pheidias may have counselled enlargement of the temple's width in order to give more fitting room for the colossal gold and ivory statue of Athena that no doubt he had already envisaged for her sanctuary.

Still another consideration in Pericles' action – and quite possibly a dominant one – was both political and economic in aim. The revised scheme for the temple was to cover an area more than a third greater than before, with a corresponding increase in volume for the marble of its construction. The change represented a formidable increase in cost, especially if the value of the gold plates and carved ivory for a 30 foot cult statue were included. Unless a new source of revenue could be found to supplement the funds (now perhaps nearing exhaustion) from Kimon's victorious campaigns, Athenian resources might well prove inadequate. However, the unexpended balance of funds of the Delian League was now deposited on the Acropolis. Inasmuch as the recently concluded Peace of Kallias by ending enmity with Persia had ended also the professed reason for the League's need of funds, the money could now be expended on other uses . . . and why not for the benefit of Athens, which had imposed and collected the tribute?!* It appears that, pursuing this line of argument, tribute from the allies of the League was annulled for the year following the peace treaty with Persia, only to be resumed when Pericles encountered no effective opposition to his diversion of League funds to local use, claiming that the tribute was due to Athens to spend as she wished, since she was the centre of an empire based on the allies' allegiance. The cost of rebuilding Athena's splendid temple could now be met!

This was the economic aspect of the project. The political one followed directly from it.

As leader of the Athenian popular party, Pericles was necessarily concerned with the popular welfare, the attainment of which was even more immediately connected with the party's political support. Plutarch's report of a phenomenal activity among the working classes induced by the vigorous prosecution of Pericles' building programme has already been quoted in a previous chapter. This may have been the first, but it was by no means the last, occasion in history when a programme of public works financed from the state treasury has been employed to keep a politician or a political party in power.

* The Peace of Kallias was negotiated in the spring of 449 B.C. In the course of that same year Pericles transferred 5,000 talents from the League treasury to Athena's account. For the year 448–447 there was a moratorium in the allied tribute list.

On being enlarged from six by sixteen to eight by seventeen columns, the new plan for the Parthenon called for six additional columns for the exterior colonnade [46]. For the front and rear porticoes, where six

46. Parthenon, plan of Periclean structure

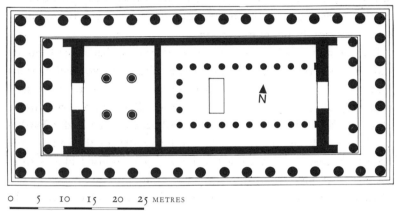

0   5   10   15   20   25 METRES

instead of four columns were scheduled for each, the problem was how best to make use of the two sets of four already mounted. Iktinos' solution was entirely logical. After resetting six of the existing eight columns at the rear portico, he decided to discard the remaining two rather than supplement them with four new ones to match. He did so because more slender proportions were then in vogue and he preferred an entire range of such columns for the entrance portico. This explains the otherwise anomalous difference between the two porticoes, in which the columns differ, not in height but in the thickness of the shafts (by as much as 6 inches or 0·152 metres, in their lower diameter). This discrepancy is perhaps the most convincing evidence for maintaining that all the columns of the Kimonian Parthenon had been erected (though of course not fluted).

It may be worth remarking that in the new Parthenon the wall-ends responding to the end columns of the porticoes were prolonged to give greater depth to the porticoes, whereas in the Kimonian version the surviving anta-base (later built into the floor of the Periclean temple) shows that the wall projection was so minimal as to reduce the anta to little more than an attached pilaster (cf. [10]). Kallikrates' use of attached pilasters has already been commented on as characteristic of his style, and may serve as one more indication that he was the architect responsible for the Older Parthenon.

Because this anta-base for the Older Parthenon had once been set and clamped into place, it follows that the flight of two shallow steps on top of which the moulded wallbase and the sanctuary wall itself were to be erected, was also already in place. This was observed many years ago by B. H. Hill in his celebrated article 'The Older Parthenon', in which he remarked that 'the lower step of the cella of the present Parthenon is composed in large part of re-used blocks from the earlier temple. This is shown . . . by the fact that they have two sets of clamp cuttings'. In addition he pointed out that these same blocks are measurable as 6 feet (1·97 metres) in length by the older footrule, but do not conform intelligibly to the 'Periclean' foot used by Iktinos. Hence they belonged originally to the Kimonian Parthenon. (*See also* Note 6 on page 175.)

Besides the exterior flight of steps, the columns of the peristyle linked by their epistyles, the front and rear portico columns on their steps, and the base of the sanctuary walls, there must have been assembled on the working site, either roughly shaped or in semi-final form ready for setting, a very considerable volume of marble blocks from the quarries of Mt Pentelikon – even though there seems to be no way of calculating how great this supply may have been.

This, then, as far as can be determined by direct measurement and indirect conjecture, describes the condition of the Parthenon at the time Kallikrates was removed from office and Iktinos undertook to rebuild the rather less than half-completed temple to a new, much larger plan. His immediate task, preliminary to erecting the New Parthenon, was to dismantle the Old.

All the forty columns of the exterior colonnade, together with their epistyles in so far as these were already in place, had to be taken down, drum by drum. (All but two corner columns of the Parthenon are put together from eleven cylindrical sections.) Here the main difficulty was not in disengaging the drums, but in shifting and rebuilding the wooden scaffolding needed to support the weight of the drums as they were lifted free, swung to one side, and lowered to the platform. If it is objected that this was an overdifficult or at any rate highly improbable procedure for masons unequipped with modern devices for dealing with heavy loads, it should be taken into account that, only a few centuries later, a completely finished temple (that of Ares) was dismembered, block by block, and successfully rebuilt in a new location. In comparison with this achievement, dismounting and re-assembling the rough hewn drums of the Kimonian Parthenon, which had no delicate flutings that might be chipped or marred, was a relatively simple matter.

If further objection is raised that Iktinos should at least have left the sixteen columns of the south flank standing and thereby spared himself the gratuitous labour of moving them, a reply will be found in the previous chapter where it was pointed out that firstly, the interval between these columns had to be lessened if seventeen columns were to be accommodated to the existing platform, and secondly, the presence of a bottom step in brown limestone instead of white marble was clearly objectionable to Iktinos, who made the best out of an awkward situation by leaving Kallikrates' steps in position along the south flank and concealing them beneath a new flight in marble. Since the exterior columns of a Greek temple are invariably based on the topmost step of the surrounding exterior flight (termed on this account the *stylobate*, i.e. 'column-walk'), none of the existing columns could remain where Kallikrates had placed them.

It is possible that still another consideration prompted Iktinos' decision to dismount the entire Kimonian peristyle. In order to clarify this, it will be necessary to consider rather fully two of the extraordinary subtleties of Periclean architecture. There is, in the first place, the well-known (but no less astonishing) property that all the horizontal lines of the Parthenon, from bottom step to cornice, have been drawn on a very gentle, yet visually detectable as well as mechanically measurable, upswelling curve rising from each of the four corners of the structure to the approximate mid-point of each of the sides.

The upper surface of the masonry platform for the temple was not precisely horizontal but rose slightly higher towards the west and south, making the south-west corner its highest point. Although the discrepancy was nowhere more than a couple of inches, it was sufficiently pronounced to cause the curvature of the superposed steps to rise a trifle more sharply from the east than from the west. Rather than ascribe the resulting asymmetry of the curves to carelessness or indifference on the part of the architect and his masons, it should be taken as a proof of extraordinary skill that they succeeded in laying out so nearly uniform curvatures on an imperfectly level foundation. Judging from available modern surveys, it would appear that the southern half of the platform was not relevelled, leaving its western end slightly higher than the eastern. On the north the platform was widened by extending the existing foundations in the western portion and cutting down the bedrock of the Acropolis at the east, making the new north-east corner of the platform exactly level with the south-east corner, and building up the new north-west corner to a height proportionately intermediate between the north-east and the higher south-west corner.

This may seem very involved to the casual reader; but the procedure assured a completely uniform curvature for the stylobate of the eastern (or principal) façade, and for the opposite western façade an almost equally symmetrical curve, while the unevenness in the curvature of the long northern flank would not have been perceptible. But on the corresponding south flank (which was least likely to be inspected by the visitor to the Acropolis) the stylobate would have had to show an asymmetrical curve that rose more sharply, if only by a couple of inches, from the east than from the west.

Partly because of this difference in curvature on the two long sides of the temple, and partly because the increment of the various curves was so minute in relation to their length (amounting to less than 5 inches in 237 feet; 0·127 metres in 72·30), it has more than once been maintained that the curves, though real, are purely accidental, being due either to imperfectly controlled workmanship or to a settling of the platform in the course of the centuries. But the latter claim is unfounded because the north-east and the south-east corners are at the same level although one is bedded on bedrock while the other rests on twenty-two courses of masonry; and further, if any settling had occurred it should not have been at the corners, where the weight of the superstructure is less. That the curvature cannot be ascribed to accident or oversight is indicated by its geometric coherence and definitely proven by the manner of construction of a comparable curvature in the contemporary Propylaea. There the stylobate is level, without rise and fall (presumably because the central processional passageway would have broken into it), but the columns of the façade are of varying height, rising from either end of the row towards the central span and thus producing a curvature in the entablature which they carry. Consequently, the curve must have been carefully planned and could not possibly have been unintentional.

A second architectural peculiarity of the Parthenon – though not peculiar in the exclusive sense of something not to be found in any other Greek temple – is the inward inclination of the columns. Instead of being exactly vertical to the plumbline, the columns on all four sides of the temple are tilted very slightly inward. In a height of about 34 modern feet (or exactly 32 ancient 'Olympic' feet of 0·326 metres) there is an inclination of about 3 inches (0·076 metres). This deviation from the vertical axis has never been challenged as unintentional, since its existence can be detected in the bias at which the bottom face of every lowest drum of the columns has been cut. Except for the bottom and top unit of every column (this top unit carrying also the capital with its abacus), the upper and lower faces of every drum are strictly parallel to each other, with their planes running at right angles to the axis of the drum. To this succession of drums with their continually diminishing diameter, a continuous tilt was communicated by cutting the under surface of the bottom drum on a slight slant, forcing the entire column to lean inward. In addition, as a result of the curvature of the stylobate, the under surface of every bottom drum had to be slanted also, though much less steeply, to a different plane lying at right-angles to that which communicated the inward tilt to the column. Similar adjustments had to be made on the upper surface of the abacus of the column capital so as to bring it level with the under side of the epistyle. As Professor Dinsmoor points out in his authoritative handbook on *The Architecture of Ancient Greece*,

These processes, in which the painstaking care bestowed upon the erection of the columns was complicated by the rising curves of the stylobate and entablature and by the inward inclination of the column axes, all entailed a mathematical precision which is almost incredible.

(However, a comment should be added that the mathematical precision was achieved empirically at the time of execution rather than by previous arithmetical or geometrical calculation.)

The results attained by means of these delicate adjustments were not invariably exact, as may be shown by comparing the spacing of the columns on the stylobate with the length of their epistyle beams at entablature height. Other irregularities between dimensions theoretically identical but actually discrepant, are relatively abundant, as in the spacing of the exterior columns which on the long flanks may vary by as much as $1\frac{3}{4}$ inches (0·043 metres). This may seem a negligibly small amount in a span of 14 feet (4·29 metres); and indeed may well be so, since the unaided eye cannot apprehend it. Nonetheless, the deviations from precision are so common in almost every structural element that the vaunted millimetric accuracy of the Parthenon may better be termed fable than 'fabulous'.

No generative formula or reconciling pattern for these deviations can be discovered – though some have occasionally been advanced. Thus it has been asserted that on the east and west façades (but not on the long flanks) the width of the metopes has been consecutively graded for 'perspective illusion' from wider metopes at the centre to narrower ones at the corners of the frieze. But graphs based on M. Balanos' measurements, show that this is not really the case, but rather that increases (perhaps casual) in the columnar intervals near the centre of the façade are necessarily reflected in an increased width of the metopes ranged above them.

Although it may seem improbable and at first encounter quite inexplicable, there clearly was no attempt at measured uniformity (or, alternatively, at any sort of rhythmic pattern) in spacing the exterior columns of the Parthenon. The irregularity is not large enough to be perceived by the spectator, since it amounts to a maximum discrepancy between adjacent columns of only about $1\frac{1}{2}$ inches (0·038 metres) on the flanks and considerably less on the ends of the temple. Yet it is this irregularity in the spacing of the columns that is responsible for the inequalities in the length of the epistyle beams, the width of the metopes, and the dimensions of the mutules and their dividing spaces (*viae*) on the underside of the projecting cornice, because the column interval is necessarily transmitted to the entablature, very much as the convex curve of the stylobate is transmitted by the columns as a parallel curvature in the entablature. Since this latter feature was deliberately introduced by the builders, it is natural to suppose that the irregular spacing of the columns was intentional also. But why should it have been?

Before trying to answer this debatable question, account must be taken of still another remarkable element in the Parthenon, namely, the extremely delicate vertical curvature in the profiles of the column shaft and its capital.

No one looking at the Parthenon can fail to notice that all the column shafts become thinner as they rise. But it takes an unusually sensitive and experienced eye to see that the thinning of the shaft does not proceed along a perfectly straight line but along a gently outward swelling arc that departs by no more than two-thirds of an inch (0·017 metres) from this straight line at any point! In the echinus (the rounded portion of the capital beneath the square abacus), the departure from a strictly straight ruled profile is so slight that the eye cannot detect it except at its upper and lower ends.

These 'refinements' (as they are generally called) were in no sense Iktinos' invention. On the contrary, they are found in greatly exaggerated form in late sixth-century Doric, where bulging columns and cushion capitals are conspicuous traits of style. From that early period onward into the later decades of the following century there was a persistent trend to less emphatic curvature until, by the period of the Parthenon and Propylaea, the cushion-shaped capital (echinus) has become an almost straight-edged spherical cone, and entasis (the counter curve to diminution in the column shaft) has all but disappeared. In view of this degenerative career, one might be inclined to judge the feeble occurrence of these features on the Parthenon as no more than habit-formed concessions to an outmoded tradition. But if one considers the extreme attention involved in laying out and actualizing these delicate deviations from simple straight profiles, it must seem highly improbable that Iktinos and his marble-cutting masons would have countenanced them without good reason.

Finally, it must not be overlooked that the outer face of the walls of the sanctuary rooms slopes inward, to echo the inward tilt of the neighbouring columns, while their interior face stands strictly vertical and their wallends (antae) again lean, but this time outward towards the column of their portico. Taken together, the deviations and non-conformities in the architectural fabric of the Parthenon are so extensive and so pervasive that more than one critic has been moved to assert (what is not quite literally true) that in the entire Parthenon there was never a straight line, either horizontal or vertical!

What can have been the architectural significance or aesthetic intention behind these intricately involved adjustments and refinements?

I think that the varieties of curvature and the inequalities of widths and spacings in the members of the Order must all be viewed together as integral parts of a single dominant idea. But to understand this idea one must be familiar with a concomitant notion that had been evolved in the intimately allied art of marble sculpture.

In our own day, Sculpture and Architecture have barely a bowing acquaintance with one another. But in the era of the Romanesque churches and Early Gothic cathedrals the sculptors and the stonemasons were a common guild of craftsmen; and in the fifth century before Christ in classic Greece their two arts were even more closely allied. Greek sculptors and builders not only worked in the same medium but used the same set of tools with the same technical procedure. From examination of marble statues that have survived in an unfinished condition it has been learned that after quarried blocks of sufficient size had been reduced to appropriate overall dimensions in rough outline, the sculptor did not proceed to cut separate parts of the figure directly into final form, each for itself, but gradually removed the entire enveloping mantle in successive and each time thinner layers, working round and round the whole figure until a completely articulated form with a finely-picked texture emerged. At this stage, metal tools were laid aside and a smooth (but not glassy or glossy) surface was created by rubbing with harder stone and sand or powdered emery. Thereafter, all details that in a living counterpart would have had colour – hair, eyeballs, lips, costume, and other inanimate accessories – were given

their approximately correct hue by working tinted wax into the pores of the marble, hence colouring but not covering or physically affecting the surface of the stone.

The stonemasons followed an identical procedure, step by step. The individual blocks out of which a complete Order was to be constructed were quarried in sufficient overall dimensions and transported to the building site on heavy carts drawn by teams of oxen. There the blocks were reduced to semi-final shape by removing superfluous stone in successive layers. Smaller units, intended for positions above the walls and epistyles – the triglyph and cornice blocks, the frames and coffers for ceiling the exterior colonnade, the marble roof tiles with their terminal antefixes – all these were tooled and trimmed to their final state before being hoisted aloft. But the column drums were left in a heavy mantle of stone to allow for channelling the knife-edged flutes running up the entire column; and the blocks for steps and walls were similarly left 'in the velvet' with as much as three-eighths of an inch of protective covering. Only when construction had been completed and there was no longer any risk of damage from moving and hoisting heavy marble, the steps and the walls were given their final dressing and smoothing of their exposed surfaces. Then, last of all, after the columns had been fluted and the profiles cut for the mouldings, colour was applied to all subsidiary detail with brightly tinted wax by the same method used for colouring statuary.

The marvellously accurate jointing which made walls and columns, though built of separate blocks, seem to have been carved out of single masses of solid stone may have been suggested, or at least influenced, by the sculptor's trick of making head and torso and limbs into a single organic whole. Whoever today in contemplating the remains of an ancient Greek temple has not sensed this congruence of the two arts, by which an assembly of many hundreds of distinguishable parts has been fused into a monolithic whole, as of sculpture, has failed to apprehend Greek architecture at its true level of attainment.

But the supreme and for the modern mind most unexpected instance of the transference of sculptural thinking to architectural practice, through an understanding of which alone the scarcely visible refinements and deliberate irregularities of the Parthenon can become intelligible, requires an extra page or two of explanation.

In the archaic phase of Greek sculpture and following thereon until the second quarter of the fifth century B.C., the artists who made marble statues depended on fixed rules of proportion by which they insured themselves against miscutting the solid block in the course of working out a human figure from it and at the same time made certain, in advance, that the proportions of this figure should be true and its anatomical detail correctly placed. These 'canonic' (i.e. measurable) rules prescribed ratios of part to part for the statuary figure in terms of simple integral numbers that could be remembered easily and readily put to use. As long afterwards as the Augustan age, Vitruvius in his treatise on Greek architecture could record that, centuries before his day, the Greek sculptors were wont to divide the heads of their statues into aliquot parts based on fixed points of reference:

For Nature has so constituted the human body that the face . . . from the bottom of the chin to the lower edge of the nostrils is a third of its height; from the nostrils to the median termination of the eyebrows the length of the nose is another third; and from this point to the springing of the hair, the forehead extends for yet another third part. . . . The rest of the bodily members have also their measured ratios, such as the ancient painters and master sculptors employed for their attainment of boundless fame.

Although Vitruvius does not list them, there were equally specific systems of proportion for the horizontal as well as the vertical axes of the human figure, such as that for the head, taken on a line passing through the tearducts of the eyes. Vitruvius' immediate reason for citing this procedure of the early Greek sculptors was to make comparison with comparable canonic rules laid down for the Ionic Order of architecture. The remarkable aspect of this comparison – which either did not strike Vitruvius or else seemed superfluous to mention – is its implicit notion that an architectural Order is in some sense a living organism like the human body.

The example given in [43] on page 101, taken from a reconstituted specimen of Pythios' Athena temple in Priene, illustrates very convincingly how a fourth-century B.C. architect could employ a canon of integral numerical ratios with complete fidelity. *But the Parthenon shows no such adherence to canonic formulae in all its parts!* The most that has been discovered is a recurrence of the proportion 9:4. This is the proportion of the length to the width of the Parthenon as measured on its top step or stylobate; and this recurs as the ratio of the height of the cornice or geison and again that of the roof gutter or sima to the height of the triglyph frieze and to that of the epistyle (these two pairs respectively having identical dimensions). This same proportion obtains between the bottom diameter of the exterior columns and the width of the triglyphs. And finally, the average axial spacing of these columns (disregarding those at the four corners of the temple, which have been moved closer to their immediate neighbours in order to accommodate the end triglyphs in proper position) stands as 9:4 to the bottom diameter of the columns on the north flank and approximates this ratio on the remaining three sides of the building. But it should be noted that the theoretical axial spacing of 4·287 metres ($\frac{9}{4}$ of the average lower column diameter of 1·90 metres) actually occurs only once in the peristyle colonnades, even though it is approached within an eighth of an inch in many instances. So close to accuracy are the inconsistent inaccuracies of column spacing! Except for this rather mysterious recurrence of a fixed proportion, all other measurements whether taken horizontally on plan or vertically in elevation yield integrally incommensurable values.

The persistent diversities in the axial spacing of the columns might be dismissed as workman's error without further significance, were it not that vastly more precise measurements such as those involved in adding the subtle curve of entasis to the straight diminution of the column shafts and giving these their inward inclination, or working the long slow curvature of the stepped stylobate, were all executed with amazingly slight deviation from mathematical precision. The only logically defensible conclusion would appear to be that there was some sort of deliberate intention behind the patternless inconsistencies of the column spacings with their consequent irregularities in the width of the metopes of the frieze and the mutule blocks of the cornice.

The only explanation that I can suggest for this apparently purposeless and yet seemingly intentional blurring of the rhythmic beat of the rigidly prescribed sequences of the Doric Order would be that Iktinos was applying to architecture the current practices of the sculptors of his time. In particular he must have been influenced by the work of Polykleitos, who (except perhaps for Pheidias) was the most important artistic personality of his generation.

In the second quarter of the fifth century the traditional formulae of the archaic phase, with their strict repetition of set patterns and schematic shapes, were being discarded by the sculptors as they came to realize that with these they were producing only geometrical abstractions and not images of living bodily forms. Although more and more complex numerical schedules could be devised to yield ever closer approximations to natural truth, the result was still an ideal and unreal construction that failed to infuse animate life to lifeless stone or bronze.

This must have been the meaning of Polykleitos' remark (presumably made in his lost treatise on his sculptural canon) that 'the employment of a great many numbers would almost produce perfection in sculpture'.

The significance of this observation is hidden in the seemingly unimportant qualification '*almost*'. By applying an elaborate series of simple integral ratios it is possible to build up a coherent structure for an ideal figure; but every one of these measurements must then be tempered by irregularity if the result is to reproduce natural physical actuality which never is geometrically true or symmetrically exact.

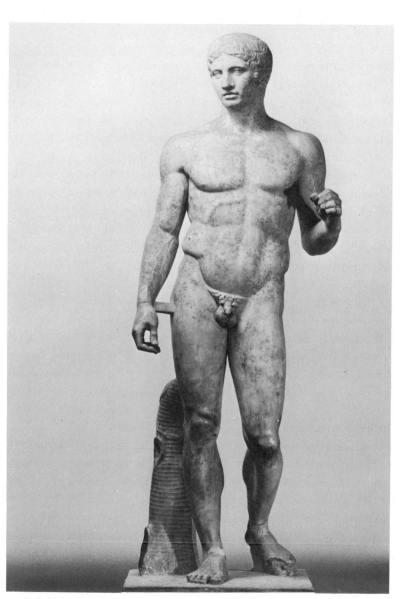

48. Polykleitos' Doryphoros, Roman copy

Accordingly, when we take most careful measurements of our copies of Polykleitos' Doryphoros [48], which we know to have embodied his canon of proportions, we fail to elicit any scheme of numerical harmony through all its parts – just as careful measuring of the Parthenon fails to yield integrally perfect ratios between its parts. The 'many numbers' have been blurred, the constructional straight lines have been tempered into curves, and lifeless geometry has been converted into more animate form.

The argument holds that, on the supposition that the theories of Polykleitos were well known to him, Iktinos applied them to architecture in the belief that the organic body of a temple would remain lifeless, like an archaic statue, unless and until it were animated by tempering its geometric rigidity with minute deviations from schematic uniformity, like those the sculptors introduced to bring their statues to life. That these irregularizing refinements of the Parthenon are mostly invisible, in that the spectator does not directly apprehend them for what they are, in no way prevents them from being effective.

But it must be admitted that even if this hypothesis is accepted as correct, it does not explain all the architectural 'refinements' of the Parthenon. To be specific, the slightly thicker columns at the four corners of the peristyle cannot be ascribed to deliberately random deviation from the norm, but must have some different aesthetic reason. Vitruvius maintained that corner columns should be made sturdier because, with more of their circumference illuminated, they would be 'eaten' by the light and hence seem thinner than they actually were. I very much doubt whether this purely optical explanation is valid. Rather, I imagine that the temple builders felt that, because a corner column did double duty by serving in two ranks, this should be emphasized visually by making it somewhat thicker and therefore stronger. Alternatively, the architects may have strengthened the corner support in a colonnade with much the same idea that led them to set exceptionally large well-cut blocks for the quoins of their walls.

As for the inward lean of the columns, I suspect that this was nothing more than an uncritical transference of the masons' long-tested tradition that if a wall is to stand up, it must be built with a batter.

These explanations, based on technical considerations, are not favoured by modern commentators, who prefer the Vitruvian thesis of correction of illusionary optical effects. Thus, we read in our standard textbook on classical Greek architecture, W. B. Dinsmoor's *The Architecture of Ancient Greece*, that the curvature of the stylobate and entablature was intended 'to prevent an appearance of sagging', which a level line is supposed to produce, while 'the convex curve to which the entasis of the columns was worked' was designed 'to correct the optical illusion of concavity which might have resulted if the sides had been straight', and 'the slight inward inclination of the axes of the columns' was 'to give the whole building an appearance of greater strength' – and this 'in spite of modern experiments made with the purpose of demonstrating that the optical illusions, which these refinements were supposed to correct, might not actually have occurred'. (In the closing phrase of this sentence I should prefer to read '*would not* actually have occurred'!)

Except, perhaps, for the reason assigned to the inward inclination of the columns, these explanations can hardly be accepted as correct.

In typical late sixth-century examples the entasis of the columns is so exaggerated that no 'optical illusion of concavity' can possibly have been under consideration. Nor could such extreme convexity have been the result of copying in stone the wooden columns of an earlier period, since tree trunks, however trimmed and shaped, would not exhibit this peculiarity. Perhaps the intrusion of entasis in heavily loaded pillars should be explained as a half consciously expressed visualization of the column's reaction to its superimposed load, much as though a man weighted down by a heavy sack might be bent under his burden yet carry it without stumbling or falling to the ground. The bulge in the early cushion capitals might have a similar explanation: note in this

49. Parthenon, east façade

50 (*opposite*). Parthenon, west façade

connexion our use of the word 'cushion', even though this was not the meaning of the Greek term *echinos*. But in the course of the fifth century the boldly emphatic bulge of the earlier column shafts and capitals had been reduced so nearly completely that it no longer forced itself on the spectator's attention. These two features must therefore have lost their original significance (whatever that may have been) and survived in the Parthenon only because they fitted into Iktinos' theory that straight profiles should be tempered to barely visible curves. (*See* Note 7 on page 177.)

So, in ten years of extraordinary activity, the Parthenon was completed in all its intricacy of lightly arched lines and scarcely perceptible irregular spacings [49 and 50]. There remained only the carving of the

wallcrown frieze on the two long flanks and the filling of the pediments at either end of the temple with statuary figures when, in 438 B.C., the dedication of Athena's new and splendid dwelling was solemnly celebrated. Far smaller in every dimension than most of the Gothic cathedrals of western Christendom, the Athenian temple in white Pentelic marble might fitly be compared to a brilliantly coloured casket enclosing a precious relic of ivory and gold. As once it stood, intact and entire, with its deceptively monolithic columns and walls, its exquisitely carved and brilliantly coloured mouldings and figured friezes, it should be rated as a sculptural masterpiece quite as much as an architectural triumph.

More than five hundred years later, Plutarch was to record of the buildings of the Acropolis that 'in their freshness and vigour they look as if they had been built only yesterday. A kind of perennial bloom preserves them from the touch of time, as though an enduring spirit of deathless life possessed them.'

In 438–437 B.C., with the Parthenon structurally complete and only the sculptors' contributions still outstanding, the crowd of skilled marble and metalworkers, with their tools and mechanical equipment, were free to take up employment on another project. Their supervising master-builder and designer, Iktinos, was likewise now disengaged, since Pheidias in his role of general superintendent of all Periclean enterprises (as Plutarch termed him) would have had supervision of the final sculptural additions to the otherwise completed temple.

In agreement with this estimate of the situation we find that the official accounts of the treasurers of Athena record disbursements for the Parthenon during the decade from 448–447 to 438–437 B.C. but in 437–436 divert their funds to the construction of a new monumental entrance gateway for the Acropolis, the magnificently planned Propylaea [51, 52 and 53]. Then, in the year 434–433 B.C., the treasurers once more assign funds for the Parthenon as wages for the sculptors (of the

51. Modern ascent to the Acropolis

pediments) and in the following year the accounts are closed, there being no further expenditure for the completed temple. In the following year, 433–432 B.C., as we learn from other sources, work on the Propylaea also ceased, leaving the splendid gateway building as near completion as it was destined ever to become. It is usually assumed that the outbreak of the great war with Sparta put an end to all construction on the Acropolis; but this supposition fails to explain why work on the Propylaea was not resumed later. It was possible to build the little Nike temple during the early years of the war, after the terrible plague had ended; and there was a five-year truce between the first and second period of open hostility, when work on the Propylaea might have been resumed. It has also been maintained that opposition from the priests of Artemis, whose sanctuary would have been curtailed by construction of the Propylaea's inner southern wing, blocked further execution

52 (*opposite*). Propylaea, interior gateway

53. Propylaea, east façade

of the original plan. This may have been a pretext put forward at the time; but the true explanation and the real reason for prevention of all continuance of the perfectly explicitly-planned project in any subsequent decade of the century was the death of Pericles from plague shortly after the outbreak of war and the consequent collapse of popular-party control, with the concurrent return of the 'Kimonian' aristocratic minority opposition to dominant power.

What, then, of Iktinos?

It may seem quite unaccountable that he was not chosen to be the architect of the Propylaea. By 438 B.C. he had completed his great task of building the Parthenon and (as we learn from reliable sources) construction of the Propylaea was begun in the following year. Why, then, was he not entrusted with this second important project for the Athenian Acropolis? In 437 B.C. Pericles was still at the height of his power; and we have no reason to suppose that Iktinos, at the brilliant consummation of his career in completing the Parthenon, stood in lesser favour with Pericles. Why, then, was the Propylaea not assigned to him as supervising architect, instead of to an unknown master named Mnesikles?

I believe that this apparent anomaly can easily be explained. On completing his work on the Parthenon Iktinos was entrusted with a commission that promised to outrank the Propylaea in importance. Hence the latter project was put in charge of Iktinos' chief assistant for the Parthenon (a connexion that may be inferred from the close resemblance of the Propylaea to the Parthenon in the proportions of its Order and characteristic features in its construction) while Iktinos himself, though he may well have had much to do with laying out the Propylaea plan, shifted his attention to nearby Eleusis, the sacrosanct cult centre of Demeter, which for many years had been under Athenian political control.

The worship of Demeter and Persephone, with its symbolic lore of the practice of agriculture, had survived through 3,000 years from neolithic times when a knowledge of ploughing, sowing, and reaping grain first reached the Greek mainland. Neoptolemos, the mythical first ploughman; Persephone, the spirit of the seed lurking under earth; and Demeter, the goddess of the ripened wheat, were still remembered at Eleusis and their gift to mankind was celebrated in a mystery masque periodically rehearsed in the presence of those who had been initiated in their cult.

The Eleusinian sanctuary is situated thirteen miles west of Athens, beyond a nearby low mountain range and beside a deep bay of the Saronic Gulf of the Aegean. The site has been subjected to repeated excavational campaigns, culminating in the removal of all the accumulated soil on its central rocky floor where once the Hall of Mysteries stood. The bewildering maze of rock-cuttings thus revealed [54] is most discouraging to the casual visitor not previously initiated into its

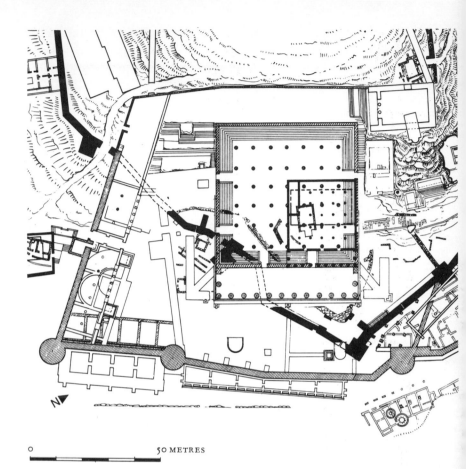

N

0   50 METRES

54. Eleusis, sanctuary, ground plan of excavated area

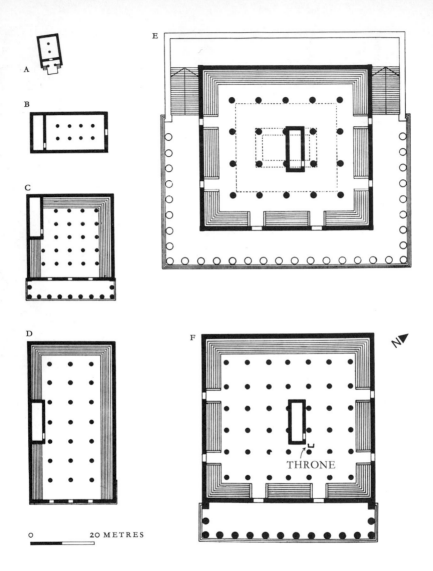

THRONE

N

O   20 METRES

55. Eleusis, sanctuary, ground plans of successive projects for the Telesterion

complexities. Yet order has been brought out of chaos by sorting chronologically the successive evidence with its mute testimony of columns, walls and tiers of seats revealing a series of ever-changing and seldom long-enduring plans. Only the last of these – labelled 'F' in the ground plan [55] – was destined to survive unsuperseded, maintaining itself intact, except for occasional repair in Roman times, until barbarian invasions and Christian hostility finally put an end to the age-old worship of Demeter and Persephone.

It is difficult to date the successive assembly halls of the Eleusinian sanctuary, but there can be no doubt about their sequence. The modest Project B [55] may be ascribed to the time of Solon, and dated to the first decade of the sixth century, while Project C represents an enlargement made later in the same century. The building must have been sacked by the Persian invaders of 480–479 and may well have lain in ruins until Kimon caused Project D to be carried out (perhaps at about the time that Kallikrates began the Parthenon). It was surely in use in Kimon's lifetime. But Pericles – as at the Parthenon – abandoned this Kimonian building and chose his own architect, Iktinos, to create a still larger and finer structure. Nothing appears to have been done until some time after 437 when the Parthenon was completed and skilled workmen were available for Eleusis. Very soon, however, work was once again suspended, as a result of the Peloponnesian war and death of Pericles.

But although it was never built – and this failure must be accounted one of the great tragedies of ancient architecture – and despite the fact that Iktinos left the already completed Kimonian hall intact while he began work outside the old fabric, traces of rock cuttings for bedding column bases make it possible to reconstruct his plan: Project E. With a truly Michelangelesque contempt for small-scale enterprises, he envisaged a columnar festal hall of about 18,000 square feet, to accommodate some 2,400 people, with a ceiling supported on columns more than fifty feet high. He seems also to have planned an exterior peristyle of thirty-two Doric columns on the same scale as those of the Parthenon.

If built, it would surely have been one of the most impressive works of Greek architecture. However, the only object which survives from Iktinos' brief period at Eleusis is the large and superbly-carved marble relief of Demeter, Persephone and a nude youth, presumably Triptolemos, the mythical first ploughman [56]. This work in the loftily beautiful yet humanly serene Pheidian manner clearly dates from the late 430s. It was presumably used in the final structure (Project F in [55]) which had much in common with Iktinos' plan, though much less imaginative and daring – it has forty-two smaller Ionic columns to support the ceiling and, outside, a portico on the south face only.

The anti-Periclean rancour, that had put an abrupt end to Iktinos' architectural career in Attica, was visited with even greater violence on the unfortunate head of Pheidias, who had been Pericles' chief adviser for the artistic beautification of Athens. He was brought to trial on a trumped-up charge of having appropriated some of the gold provided for the colossal cult statue of Athena in the Parthenon. According to the account in Plutarch's *Life of Pericles*, 'as the prosecution proceeded, nothing of theft or embezzlement was proved against him; for he had so wrought and cast the gold for the statue that it might be removed again and completely weighed'. This accusation having come to naught a charge of impiety was next directed against Pheidias for having 'introduced a likeness of himself' in the representation of the battle of Greeks and Amazons on Athena's decorated shield. The outcome, according to Plutarch, was that Pheidias 'was conveyed to prison and died there of disease or, as some say, of secretly administered poison'.

It is, of course, entirely possible that Pheidias was imprisoned on one charge or another; but he certainly did not die there, since (whether through reprieve or connived flight or his own free act) he moved to Olympia to erect a colossal chryselephantine statue of Zeus in the god's temple. Although this temple had been built some thirty years before, either it had stood without a cult image in its interior or, much more probably, contained the antiquated one from the temple of Hera, now

56. Demeter, Persephone and Triptolemos, marble relief

to be replaced by a magnificent new statue comparable in size to the gold-and-ivory Athena of the Parthenon.

Perhaps as early as 430 B.C. Pheidias established his workshop in the sacred close of Olympian Zeus, having brought with him, we may assume, the most skilful of the artisans who had been associated with him on the Athena Parthenos. And thither, in all likelihood, came also Iktinos to assist by building the great timbered armature for the statue with its scaffolding and accomplishing the other tasks of resetting the inner floor of the temple with white marble bordered by black Eleusinian limestone and placing the stone screens which Pheidias' brother, Panainos, was to decorate with paintings of mythological themes, and lastly to supervise the engineering incident to erecting on its ornate pedestal the forty-five foot statue of the seated god.

It is true that we have no direct knowledge that Iktinos joined Pheidias in Olympia; but his residence in Olympia seems confirmed by the reminiscences of Olympian architecture to be seen in the temple of 'Aid-bringing Apollo', high in the Arcadian hills a long day's journey on foot from low-lying Olympia. Here in a secluded upland glen (whence the name Bassai) Iktinos designed what seems to have been the last work of his life [57].

Our only authorization for ascribing the temple to Iktinos is the passage in Pausanias' *Guide to Greece*, written in the second century of the Roman Empire, containing a brief but categoric statement:

Next to the temple at Tegea it is the most highly praised of all the Peloponnesian temples for the beauty of its marble and its fine construction. It derives its name from Apollo as having come to the rescue against the plague at the time of the war between the Peloponnesians and Athenians . . . as is evidenced by the fact that the architect of the temple was Iktinos, who was a contemporary of Pericles and built the Parthenon for the Athenians.

It has at times been suggested that Pausanias must have been misinformed and that the ascription of the temple to Iktinos was due to local

57. Temple of Apollo Epikourios, Bassai

58

58–61. Temple of Apollo Epikourios, Bassai, details of frieze

60

59

vainglory, desirous of attaching a famous name to the remote and little visited temple. But the frieze [58, 59, 60 and 61] from the interior room (the renowned 'Phigaleian frieze' of the British Museum) and the fragmentary metopes [62] from the entrance portico are of unmistakable Attic workmanship from the 420s B.C. and, even more conclusively

61

62. Temple of Apollo Epikourios, Bassai, metope

(because not subject to importation from elsewhere), some of the mouldings could have been designed and carved only by Athenian artisans
of this same period. Presumably these masons had accompanied Iktinos
to Olympia and thus were available – as was Iktinos himself – for an
out-of-the-way commission inland in south-western Arcadia.

The temple of Apollo Epikourios at Bassai, though now without
ceilings or roof, shows most of its columns in place, with its walls re-
erected and scattered specimens of its superstructure lying close at
hand [63 and 64]. But this fullness of architectural information only
serves to emphasize the peculiarities that set Bassai apart from all other
Greek temples known to us.

63. Temple of Apollo Epikourios, Bassai, general view

64. Temple of Apollo Epikourios, Bassai, exterior columns

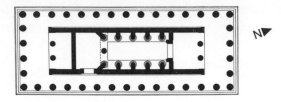

65. (*above*) Temple of Apollo Epikourios, Bassai, ground plan, contrasted with (*below*) Parthenon, plan of Periclean structure, at same scale

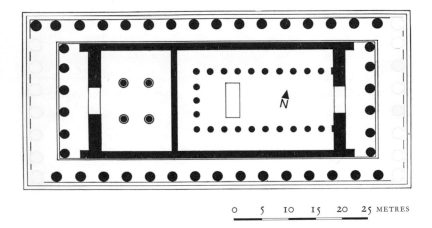

0   5   10   15   20   25 METRES

66. Temple of Apollo, Delphi, ground plan, at same scale as above plans

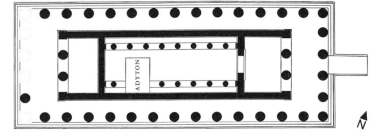

To begin with the plans [65]: the abnormally broad space in front of exceptionally deep vestibules absorbs three-fifths of the temple platform's total length, leaving considerably less than half that length for the sanctuary itself with its added inner chamber (opposite above). This arrangement of plan contrasts markedly with that of the Parthenon (opposite centre), in which very shallow porticoes opening off an extremely narrow ambulatory leave proportionately far more space available for the interior. On the other hand, the Hephaisteion much more closely resembles Bassai in plan. But the closest analogy is with Apollo's own greater temple at Delphi [66], which, as at Bassai, attains greater length by setting fifteen instead of the thirteen columns canonic for a six-column front. And that it was this temple of Apollo at Delphi, and not the Hephaisteion in Athens, from which the designer of the Bassai temple took his plan is proven by the fact that the stylobate (the top step on which the columns stand) at Bassai measures almost precisely, within an inch or two, two-thirds that of the Delphic temple and makes the same use of the two extra column-intervals to add a second inner room – at Delphi to house Apollo's oracle, at Bassai for a purpose unknown.

This inner room at Bassai has given rise to considerable speculation. It can hardly have had an oracular function, like the adyton at Delphi, because it was not shut off from the rest of the temple, but entirely accessible, not only from the main sanctuary but also from the outside colonnade by way of a separate doorway through the temple wall. Inasmuch as the temple is (very exceptionally) oriented to front the north instead of the eastern horizon, it is this inner chamber from which the line of sight, through the unusual doorway and the interval between two of the exterior columns of the peristyle, is directed toward the east. Because of this it has been supposed that the cult statue of the god was set against the west wall of this inner sanctum so that it might face the sunrise and behold the sacrificial rites performed at the god's altar outside. But there are no traces of such an altar; and it has been objected that the floor paving of the chamber has not been laid out to suggest that a statue ever stood in the assumed location.

But this inner room is in no sense the most peculiar feature of this interesting temple. Far more surprising and in some respects most completely baffling is the architectural disposition of the main interior. Instead of a central nave flanked by colonnaded aisles, as in the Hephaisteion and other Greek temples of comparably narrow width, half-columns terminating short spur walls create a series of niche-like compartments, thereby blocking and eliminating the continuous aisles that might have been expected [65 and 67]. This treatment of the interior

67. Temple of Apollo Epikourios, Bassai, sanctuary

appears to have been copied from the archaic temple of Hera at Olympia. Not so the attached half-columns that rise from a completely unparalleled type of flaring Ionic base [68] and carry an even stranger looking three-

68. Temple of Apollo Epikourios, Bassai, detail of columns

69. Temple of Apollo Epikourios, Bassai, interior

faced Ionic capital. The drawing here reproduced as [69] shows a
reconstruction of the interior of the temple by an experienced German
architect, Fritz Krischen.

As the illustration makes apparent, the attached Ionic half-columns
supported a smooth-faced epistyle surmounted by an elaborately sculptured frieze, above which a cornice crown carried a marble coffered
ceiling across the entire room. The entablature with its frieze was
carried around the four sides of the room. Where it crossed above the
entrance doorway at the north end, it was given adequate support by a

lintel of double width; but at the other end of the sanctuary, where this opened on the inner chamber, the 17 foot span between the end columns was judged too great for an otherwise unsupported marble beam. In consequence, a central prop was introduced in the shape of a lone free-standing column. This was not given the awkwardly flaring base of the rest of the series nor yet its inconveniently trifaced capital.

On the evidence of sketches and drawings made by the German architect Haller at the time of the first modern study of the temple site in 1811 and 1812, it is known that the capital of this central column [70], no longer extant, resembled the Corinthian classical norm [71] in having the bottom of its cylindrical drum encircled by a double row of acanthus leaves with long curling tendrils springing from them to meet under the corners of the square crowning abacus, while other shorter tendrils met to fill the intervening spaces – a complicated description, but the standard Corinthian capital is a very complex creation!

As far as we know at present, the first fully evolved Corinthian capital in the fixed tradition of Graeco–Roman architecture is the builder's sample (*paradeigma*) that was buried in the foundations of the exquisite round tholos at the sanctuary of Aiskulapios near Epidauros [71]. When this is set beside Haller's drawing of the lost capital at Bassai [70] one can hardly conclude otherwise than that the latter, dating from the second previous architectural generation,* is the direct ancestor of the classic Epidauran type; so that whoever designed the Bassai capital may be claimed to have been the originator of the Corinthian Order. But to assume that this creative designer was Iktinos directly contradicts the tradition current in Antiquity that claimed this distinction for an Athenian sculptor of the Pheidian school, named Kallimachos, and held that the capital was called Corinthian because it was invented by him at

* The tholos of Epidauros is listed by Pausanias as the work of Polykleitos the Younger, almost certainly the grandson of the famous sculptor who was approximately contemporary with Iktinos.

Corinth. And, of course, Kallimachos might have accompanied his master, Pheidias, to Olympia and in turn moved with Iktinos to Bassai (though this assumption throws no light on his connexion with Corinth).

It may seem illogical and even unaccountable that Iktinos should have set a uniquely different capital on the lone central pillar at the rear of the sanctuary of the Bassai temple when he might perfectly well have used a normal Ionic one to carry the entablature with its frieze across the span. An explanation for his action is ready at hand.

70 (*opposite*). Drawing of capital of interior column
from temple of Apollo Epikourios, Bassai

71. Capital from sanctuary of Aiskulapios, Epidauros

On examining the notebooks of the architects who visited the temple
in 1812, Professor Dinsmoor noted that in their excavation of the site
they had uncovered pieces of another 'Corinthian' capital (or capitals)
in addition to the intact existing one; and Professor Dinsmoor himself
during a study of the ruins of the temple in the late 1920s had observed
cuttings in the capping stones of the diagonal spur walls made to accommodate capitals of this shape. It follows that not only the lone central
column but also the two diagonal spur walls confronting it once carried

capitals of this type. These were employed for the simple and sufficient reason that neither the ordinary Ionic capital nor yet the peculiar three-faced form crowning the other spur walls would have met the requirements of a position where an entablature turned at a right-angle over a wall aligned on a 45° diagonal bias. What Iktinos needed in order to meet this unusual situation was a capital without fixed orientation or alignment; and this he supplied with his 'proto-Corinthian' invention.

Hereby Iktinos had found a remedy for an otherwise extremely inconvenient defect in the traditional Ionic capital. Just as no classical colonnade can ascend or descend a slope or otherwise adapt itself to a change of level because it is tied to the gravitational mechanics of a horizontal load on a vertical support, so an Ionic colonnade, unlike its Doric counterpart, cannot even change direction without becoming involved in difficulties with its capital. Over the angle column, where two ranges of entablature meet at 90°, it is impossible to carve volutes on the two adjoining faces of the capital without their mutual interference; and the opposing bolsters, meeting in the inside corner, do even greater damage to each other. The need was for a capital without fixed orientation, that would be cylindrical where it rose from the column shaft and rectilinear where it supported the epistyle – in short, a capital like the Corinthian.

It is usually stated that there were three classical Greek Orders. This is not true: until Imperial Roman times, there were only two Orders, the Doric and the Ionic, with the latter possessing a variant form of capital, which (for reasons unknown to us) Antiquity elected to call Corinthian. This alternate form was devised in order to eliminate the above-mentioned defects in the traditional type. And if, as seems most probable, it was Iktinos who resolved the difficulty, he would belong in the front rank of the ancient architects, if for that reason alone.

There remains one more problem that has perplexed all who have visited Bassai or read about it. At the inner end of the sanctuary room, diagonal spur walls jut out [65] from the main temple wall on either side, to help enclose a niche-like bay of awkward shape with an unsightly inner corner. More objectionable still, from the point of view of intelligent and intelligible planning, are the cupboard-like nooks that flank the entrance doorway. Shall we not have to accuse Iktinos of inexpert designing and judge this to be an old man's lapse from his former intellectual strength?

The ancient temple of Hera at Olympia employed this same device of interrupting the side aisles with spur walls projecting at a right angle from the main enclosing wall of the temple; but there the spurs were spaced and aligned in exact agreement with the columns of the outer peristyle, whereas at Bassai the similar spur walls, although spaced at the same interval as the columns of the exterior colonnade, are aligned with the mid-point of these columns' open interval. Now, mere inspection of the plan will reveal that if these same five spur walls had been centred on the peristyle columns, as in the Heraion, the number of niches would have remained the same, but they would all have been of equal size and shape, and the two irregularly-outlined bays and the two minuscule nooks, so objectionable in the present plan, would never have existed.

It would seem, therefore, that an original plan, based on that of the Heraion at Olympia, was superseded by the present internal arrangement, which resulted from shifting the spur walls northward in the direction of the entrance doorway by half the amount of an intercolumniation of the outer peristyle; and that this was done in order to gain just that amount of additional space for the area of the inner chamber. If only we knew (or could properly conjecture) what function this chamber was intended to perform, we should be in a position to judge whether this hypothesis was correct. And in case it proved right, we should probably shift the blame for illogical and unsatisfactory planning from Iktinos to the unenlightened interference of the priestly authorities. Bassai would then become our earliest known instance of a client's opinionated ideas ruining an architect's carefully considered plan.

For final observation it should be recorded that at Bassai the stylobate below and the entablature above the columns shows no horizontal curvature, as in the Parthenon, and that the walls and columns are not built of lucent white marble but of dull grey local limestone, harsh and brittle and difficult to work. No doubt the reason for both of these economies was lack of available funds. Like many another architect in the history of art, Iktinos was balked in his ambitions by an ungenerous exchequer. Nonetheless he managed to introduce a slight entasis into the tapering column shafts and, perhaps in reminiscence of his Athenian days, reproduced the profile of the Parthenon's Doric capitals [26 and 72] and the Propylaea's mouldings for cornice-crown and main wallcrown so faithfully that it may be said that at Bassai the seal of late fifth-century Athens was as unmistakably stamped on the architecture as its sculptural style was writ large on the frieze within and the metopes of its entrance portico.

72. Temple of Apollo Epikourios, Bassai, capital of exterior Order

Notes

Note 1

The Substructure of the Parthenon

(see page 24)

A cross-section of these walls is shown in [73], and a plan is reproduced in [74]. These drawings should be constantly consulted while reading the following account.

In order to form a correct mental picture of this complex subterranean region, considerable visual effort may be required in combining

73. Parthenon substructure, cross-section at the east end

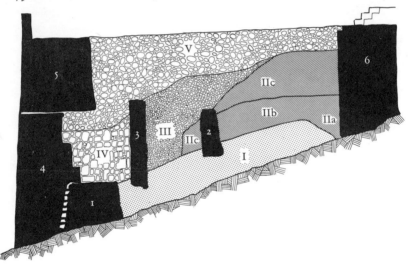

1. 'Mycenaean' circuit wall
2. Polygonal retaining wall
3. Ashlar retaining wall
4. Kimonian Acropolis wall
5. Periclean addition
6. Foundation platform of the Parthenon

the horizontal extension of the area in [74] with the vertical transverse view taken at only a single point in [73]. A useful beginning may be made by noting that the Arabic numerals in [73] recur in the legend at the upper right of [74] where the five stretches of wall are identified as 'Mycenaean', 'polygonal', 'ashlar', 'Kimonian' and 'Periclean'. The next step in this visual reconstruction proceeds from the masonry styles of the walls, which differ markedly in their manner of building and therewith give some clue to their relative ages and purposes.

Wall 1, identified as Mycenaean, is a sector of the immemorially old defensive girdle around the hilltop of the Acropolis. Whether or not it

74. Parthenon substructure, plan showing retaining walls on the south

⊞ Mycenaean (1 in plan opposite)
▒ Polygonal wall (2)
■ Ashlar terrace wall (3)
▨ Kimonian–Periclean Acropolis wall (4, 5)

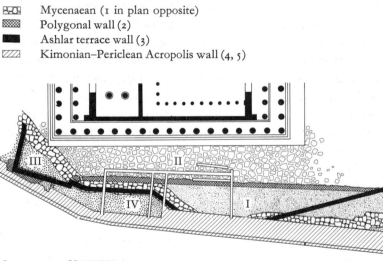

O   20 METRES

all really dates from a thousand years before the Parthenon is immaterial. Bedded on the solid rock and put together out of rudely-shaped but skilfully fitted blocks to form a rampart with average thickness of *c.* 15 feet (4·57 metres), it made up in strength what it occasionally lacked in height. Even so, at an opposite side of the Acropolis, Persian invaders detected in it a point of weakness at which they succeeded in climbing the rock, to sack and pillage Athena's sacred citadel. After the Persian army withdrew, never again to overrun mainland Greece, several years elapsed before the higher and stouter wall labelled '4' in [73] was erected. Here on the southward slope of the rocky hilltop, at a distance varying between 50 and 100 feet (15·24 and 30·48 metres) from the temple platform (and hence only roughly parallel to it), there was built outside and beyond the old circuit wall a new and much taller structure of squared blocks of limestone fitted in level courses to an average height of nearly 40 feet (12·20 metres), thereby exceeding the great platform's height (though not, of course, its bulk) although, because based much farther down the rocky slope, reaching no higher than the platform's eleventh course of masonry. This discrepancy was later annulled by the addition of an even broader wallcrown (5 in [73]), which brought the fortification wall of the Acropolis south of the Parthenon flush with the platform's top.

Walls 1, 4, and 5 have thus been dealt with, without giving rise to any apparent difficulties of interpretation. But what explanation should be given for the existence of Walls 2 and 3, which at first sight seem to have no intelligible use or purpose?

A clue is given by a seemingly minor detail of construction, observed when the two walls were uncovered. On both of them only the outside (i.e. downhill) face had been correctly aligned and finished, thereby proving conclusively that both walls were intended to serve as retaining walls to hold behind them thrown-in dump or fill, whether of soil or rubble or builders' discard, to form some kind of terracing between them and the temple platform's high masonry.

Since their manner of construction differed markedly – one being in semi-polygonal, the other in ashlar work – the two walls could hardly have been contemporary. And since in classical Antiquity the polygonal style was normally an older way of building than ashlar, and because Wall 2 would scarcely have been necessary or served any useful function if Wall 3 with its greater height had already been standing, we may conclude that Wall 2 preceded Wall 3 and that, concomitantly, Wall 3 supplanted Wall 2. Again, if Wall 3 were already functioning in support of a filled-in terrace slope, Wall 2 could not have been built; whereas with Wall 2 in place, the crown of the Mycenaean circuit wall would have remained exposed and accessible for raising Wall 3 upon it.

A similar argument supports the priority of Wall 3 to Wall 4, inasmuch as the erection of Wall 3 would have been a pointless waste of money and effort if the vastly stronger outer wall of the Acropolis had already been in place.

All this discussion would be perhaps of no more than casual archaeological interest were it not that the entire problem of the Parthenon's history and the relative roles of its two recorded architects, Kallikrates and Iktinos, hinge directly on the interpretation of this intricate underground evidence.

Note 2

The Date of the Foundations of the Parthenon

(see page 28)

To clinch this evidence it may be well to quote in full Professor Dinsmoor's categoric statement:

Among these easily datable sherds of the three last decades (of the sixth century B.C.) we obtain the following proportions: 65 per cent of about 510, and 9 per cent of about 490 B.C. This gradual diminution in the number of sherds from each decade, terminating abruptly with 490 B.C. . . . forms an indication that we are approaching the date of the foundation. It would be difficult to imagine that as many as seven important pieces (of decorated pottery) manufactured about 510 B.C. had been broken up and buried (only) four or five years later; but when we add to these the testimony of the four pieces from 500–490 it becomes increasingly clear that the fill could not have been deposited as early as 506 B.C. or immediately thereafter. If we assume for the latest vase a date about 495 B.C., it would be reasonable to assume that this single example has been accidentally broken within seven or eight years and was used as part of the fill in the V-shaped trench (stratum IIa). [This] gives us the date *post quem* for the beginning of the Parthenon foundation as about 495 B.C. or rather a few years later.

Note 3

The Ashlar Retaining Wall
(see page 37)

After making contact with the old circuit wall of the Acropolis about in line with the eastern end of the Parthenon, Wall 3 (see diagrams 73 and 74 on pages 160 and 161) was carried on top of it, along its outer edge, to the point where it bent sharply in to the platform's west corner. At this point Wall 3 parted company with the circuit wall, to pursue an independent course in the shape of a right-angle triangle, a sort of redoubt projecting outside the circuit wall's defence. Evidently there must have been some functional relation between the two walls. Yet this function cannot have been that of strengthening the defence of the Acropolis, since Wall 3 follows the circuit only for the stretch abreast of the Parthenon and, besides, is not built in comparable solidity to serve as fortification. Instead, the wall must have used the circuit wall as underpinning in order to set up a barrier against an accumulation of builders' debris and terraced fill too copious for Wall 2. And the triangular 'redoubt' finds its obvious explanation in the retreat of the circuit wall to the very corner of the platform, leaving no space for dumping or terracing. The erection of Wall 3 therefore argues a resumption of building activity on the temple platform.

Yet this activity could not have been connected with the existing Parthenon in so far as this was a Periclean enterprise begun (as we know from inscriptions and other evidence) in the year 447 B.C., whereas Wall 3 must have been set up at least a couple of decades earlier.

There is universal agreement that Wall 4 is part of the great strengthening bulwark of the Acropolis erected during the lifetime and by the initiative of the great military and political leader Kimon, and that the cost of it was defrayed from funds accruing from the spoils of the famous battle of the River Eurymedon – Kimon's most spectacular victory – to be dated close to the year 466 B.C. Plutarch in his seemingly well-documented life of Kimon expressly states that 'the Athenian people raised so much wealth from the spoils of this war, which were auctioned publicly, that in addition to other outlay they erected the south wall of the Acropolis and laid the foundation of the long walls' (between the city and its harbour of Peiraeus). Elsewhere he refers to 'the south wall of the Acropolis, built by Kimon'; and Pausanias in his *Guide to Greece* says that Kimon built the Acropolis walls in so far as these were not of legendary origin.

Now, it should further be clear that Wall 3 would have been entirely pointless and unnecessary if Wall 4 already existed (cf. [73]). Therefore Wall 3 must have preceded the great Kimonian construction, if by no more than a few years. It may be dated to the late 470s or early 460s, as is shown by a rather subtle and difficult combination of material evidence.

At the apex of the triangle of the redoubt, where Wall 3 impinges upon the Kimonian fortification, photographs made at the time this area was excavated show Wall 3 based on the bottom courses of this Kimonian wall, thereby proving that Kimon's wall had been begun before the redoubt was built. But at a higher level the situation is reversed: the upper part of Kimon's wall presupposes and relies on the redoubt wall, proving that the redoubt was completed before Kimon's more massive structure was finished. If this observation and the inferences from it are sound, it follows that the redoubt and the adjacent stretch of the Kimonian defences of the Acropolis were virtually contemporaneous, while the remainder of Wall 3 had been built previously (since, as we have seen, it would have served no purpose if the Kimonian circuit were already in place). It follows that with only a dozen years intervening between the Persian sack of Athens and the Greek victory at the Eurymedon, Wall 3 should be assigned to the latter part of the decade of the 470s or the early years of the 460s B.C.

And since the wall must have been built to hold back an accumulation of debris heaped higher than Wall 2 and stratum II, there must have been construction under way on the temple platform at least twenty years before Pericles acquired supreme control over Athens at Kimon's death in 450 B.C. and initiated the present Parthenon, with Iktinos as its master-builder, in 447.

Note 4

The Metopes from the Parthenon now in the British Museum

(see page 65)

Metope No.	*Width at bottom*	*Condition*	*Comment*
II	1·280 m.	Right end retrimmed (?) and plastered	Too short for present Parthenon
III	1·280 m.	Right end retrimmed	Too short for present Parthenon
IV	1·256 m.	Both ends cut	Too short for present Parthenon
V	1·370 m.	Left margin cut	
VI	1·295 m.	Both end-faces plaster	A trifle too short
VII	1·380 m.		Centaur without tail
VIII	1·305 m.	Left margin plaster	Centaur's tail trimmed
IX	1·334 m.	Left margin plaster	
XXVI	1·335 m.		Centaur's tail cut; lapith's drapery smoothed down for overlapping triglyph

Metope No.	Width at bottom	Condition	Comment
XXVII	1·380 m.	Right margin damaged	Drapery at left worked away for triglyph projecting
XXVIII	1·350 m.	Left end retrimmed	
XXIX	1·297 m.		Short?
XXX	1·290 m.		Centaur's hindquarter undercut for triglyph projecting behind it
XXXI	1·340 m.		Centaur's tail shaved down at base
XXXII	1·347 m.	Margins trimmed?	

Note: The average width of a metope from the south flank should be *c.* 1·34 m. if 0·040 m. is allowed for the overlap of the triglyphs.

Note 5

Other Temples by Kallikrates

(see page 102)

There is an Athenian temple which shows some remarkable similarities
to the temple on Delos, not in its physical dimensions (since it was considerably larger) but in the proportions of its members. This temple
formerly stood in the Athenian Agora, where it had been re-erected in
the reign of the Emperor Augustus after having been dismantled and
moved from some other location probably beyond the city limits. Dedicated to the war-god Ares, it was finally destroyed in late Roman times
and its pieces scattered among medieval and modern buildings, from
which a sufficient number have been recovered in the course of the
American excavation of the Agora to permit a complete and accurate
rebuilding of it (but this time on paper only!) by Professor Dinsmoor.
From his fully documented publication (*Hesperia*, vol. IX (1940) pp.
1–52) it may be gathered that the temple was originally built about
438–434 B.C. and that it was the work of the nameless architect of the
nearby temple of Hephaistos. Of significance for our present inquiry is
the fact that in its Doric Order several of the principal proportions are
practically identical with those of the corresponding elements of the
temple on Delos, as the following tabulation shows:

Ratio	Temple of Ares	Temple of Delos
of the lower diameter to the height of the columns	5·70	5·71
of the diameter of the columns to the height of the entire Order	7·520	7·526
of the height of the columns to the height of their entablature	3·142 (average)	3·15
of the height of the columns to the height of the entire Order	1·318	1·317

The only major discrepancy between the two temples is in the spacing of the columns. Those of the Ares temple were set considerably closer together relatively to their thickness.

From the above table of proportions there results a *prima facie* possibility that the architect of the Athenian temple on Delos was the same as the designer of the temple of Ares in Athens, who in turn, according to Dinsmoor's considered opinion, was the builder of the Hephaisteion! He reached this conclusion largely from the fact that, entirely disregarding the differing column heights of the Ares temple and the Hephaisteion, the entablatures that the columns carried were not related to one another in the same ratios as the column heights, thus violating the cardinal rule of constant proportions within the Order. Contrary to this rule, the entablatures of the two temples were almost precisely identical in their actual dimensions despite the discrepancy in the height and thickness of their columns.

Dinsmoor made a similar observation on yet another Attic temple, that of Poseidon on the cape of Sunion, where the columns were a foot higher than in the Hephaisteion, yet the entablature heights were the same to less than half an inch.

Had the entablatures of these three temples been *precisely* identical in all their measurements, we should have had to conclude that the builders were saving themselves the trouble of designing separate models for the masons to copy; but this is not the case. However closely the measurements agree in all three temples, they are not completely identical. The only plausible explanation must be that the architect, for reasons of personal choice and taste, considered these particular dimensions best for the superstructure of the Order, irrespective of the varying height of the supporting columns. But this is precisely the anomaly that we met previously in Kallikrates' temple of Nike where, while the other details of plan and elevation were reduced from its prototype, the Ilissos temple, by approximately 9 per cent, the entablature was reduced by little more than 1 per cent, in other words was repeated at very nearly identical absolute size.

We are here confronted by a trait or mannerism such as not infrequently distinguishes the individual craftsman from his contemporaries. When we encounter this same unusual characteristic in a number of Athenian temples, all constructed within a period of little more than twenty years, we can hardly fail to conclude that all were the work of a single man – in this case, Kallikrates.

Possibly an inference of this sort will strike the reader as somewhat tenuous and unsubstantial. Still, it will turn out to be fully supported by the second of the technical criteria advanced on a previous page, the criterion of the mouldings separating and defining the elements of the Order. The profiles of two such mouldings, taken from Dr Shoe's repertoire, are set side by side in [75]. They reproduce faithfully and at exact size the carved contour of the capitals of the wall ends (antae) and

75. Profiles of anta capitals,
(*left*) Hephaisteion, Athens, and (*right*) Temple of the Athenians, Delos

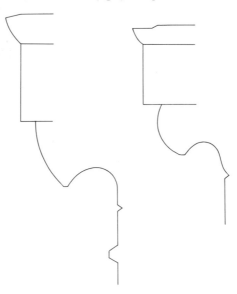

pilasters of the temple of the Athenians on Delos ([75] right) and the anta capitals of the Hephaisteion in Athens ([75] left).

There is no need to argue the evident fact that these two profiles are all but identical in every respect other than their physical size; yet the reader who examines them may not feel so fully convinced that this particular sequence of a 'hawksbeak' carrying a broad horizontal band (fascia) crowned by a small ovolo, with all three of these parts contoured and proportioned alike, may be taken as proof that one and the same architect (to be identified as Kallikrates) designed both temples. Yet consultation of Dr Shoe's folio plates will persuade the sceptic that no other close parallel to the Delos anta moulding, with the same contour and proportions, can be adduced anywhere among the surviving specimens of ancient Greek architecture!*

The only discernible divergence in the two profiles is due to an artistic innovation that took place during the twenty-year interval between their designing. The profile from the Delos temple has not been drawn or set crookedly on the page, but faithfully records a slight forward tilt in the broad fascia above the hawksbeak as well as in the start of the undercut hollow beneath it. These deviations from the strict vertical were purposely introduced in order to compensate for the foreshortening incident to viewing the anta capital from below. Such an 'optical refinement' (as the architectural handbooks call it, although 'optical correction' would here be a better term) imitates a characteristic feature of the Periclean Parthenon and Propylaea, from which Kallikrates would have learned it. From this tell-tale, albeit minute detail a specialist in this comparatively unfamiliar field of architectural study would have been able to deduce the later date of the Delos temple in relation to the Hephaisteion, because he would have recognized that the

* The south-west wing of the Propylaea offers the closest parallel; but even here the correspondence is not very close, and a different type of moulding has been employed for the small crowning member.

completion of the Periclean Parthenon must have intervened between the construction of the two temples.

Professor Dinsmoor assigns to his 'nameless architect' of the Hephaisteion (whom I have identified with Kallikrates) two other temples – that of Poseidon on the spectacular rocky headland of Sunion, and the never completed temple to Nemesis, divinity of Retribution, at Rhamnus in a remote corner of Attica close to the sea, some eight miles beyond Marathon. While the temple at Sunion recalls the Hephaisteion in a number of significant details, it adds little to the present inquiry, except for the recurrence of a wall- and anta-base moulding in the manner of the Hephaisteion and the Kimonian Parthenon.

At Rhamnus nothing remains to be seen today save a broken marble floor and the lowest drums of a few unfluted columns; but previous investigators of the site found more to examine and record. Among the peculiarities that connect this temple with the Hephaisteion the most informative for our present interest is the use of low-grade blue local marble for the foundations and bottom step of the platform in contrast to the white Pentelic marble employed for the rest of the building. It may be recalled that both the Kimonian Parthenon and the Hephaisteion made a similar distinction in the lowest member of the flight of steps. This is another link for the chain of Kallikratean temples.

The resemblance of some of the mouldings to those in corresponding positions on the Periclean Parthenon may be used as evidence that the temple of Nemesis at Rhamnus was begun later than the year 440 B.C., while the unfluted state of its columns suggests that construction was interrupted by outbreak of the Peloponnesian War in 432 because of the impossibility of defending a site so distant from the city against marauding Spartan armies. A date in the thirties therefore seems assured.

Note 6

The Epistyle Beams

(see page 114)

At Segesta in western Sicily the unfinished temple has a complete entablature on its exterior range of columns, even though the bedrock shows no sign of any cuttings for the foundations of the interior walls and columns. If the analogy holds good, we should assume that for the Kimonian Parthenon the epistyles, at least, would have been set in place to yoke together and stabilize the columns, even though it seems unlikely that any further elements of the superstructure were added. It can hardly be mere coincidence that the column cappings (abacus) of the exterior columns of the extant Parthenon, while varying somewhat from column to column, have an average width of seven of the 'older' feet, and that the epistyle that they carry in the shape of three parallel marble beams has a width of almost precisely six of these feet and a height that exceeds four and a half of these feet by barely half an inch.* Hence it may be conjectured with considerable assurance that the epistyle beams of the extant Parthenon were re-used from the Kimonian structure. It should be noted that the column spans are of slightly unequal length and that, in addition, the joints between consecutive epistyle blocks are not invariably centred on the precise axis of the column which carries them. Consequently if the Kimonian epistyles were trimmed down to fit the somewhat shortened span between

---

* The width of the abacus varies between 2·02 metres and 2·09 metres (except on the slightly thicker corner columns). 7 'older' feet of 0·2957 = 2·07 metres. The width of the three epistyle beams is 1·777 metres, 6 older feet = 1·774 metres. The height of the epistyle is 1·345 metres. 4½ older feet = 1·331 metres, a discrepancy of 0·014 metres. Only the last of these three dimensions yields plausible multiples of the 'Periclean' foot of 0·328 metres.

columns, a variety of extremely awkward difficulties would result if the outer beam already had its cleats and studs (the regulae and guttae) carved along its upper edge. However, if these adornments had been left to be cut later, after the epistyle was in place, no inconvenience would have resulted. This suggestion is not as improbable as might appear. Precisely because considerable adjustment by cutting and trimming was always involved in fitting epistyle blocks together over columns whose axial distances were bound to be irregular at that level, the half regula with its guttae that each block carried could not have been fully cut and finished in advance.

Note 7

The Doric Order

(see page 131)

In the Greek Orders, gravitational equilibrium and horizontal symmetry are very openly expressed; and it is through the formal detail of the component elements that this expression is made articulate. If the surfaces were left blank and the various structural elements were not distinguishably set off from one another, or if irrelevant ornament and decorative design were allowed to intrude on them, the aforementioned effect would no longer be visually communicable. Much of the detail of the Orders is structurally inactual and hence materially unnecessary. It exists for its aesthetic function, and pertains not to engineering but to art.

It should be apparent to every critical spectator that the Greek Orders are an assembly of abstract formal elements of pre-established shape and proportionally calculated size, that each of these elements is sharply differentiated and separated from its fellows, and that each is superficially adorned in carved and coloured design with intent of suggesting some structural function contributory to the total constructional scheme. It is significant that this structural function is far more frequently only *suggested* and seldom literally performed. Thus, in the complex assembly of squared and closely-fitted blocks of marble or limestone which a Greek Order presents, a column base between platform and column shaft is not structurally required (as the Doric norm concedes); the capital (though perhaps not its abacus) could be omitted without weakening the column-support; the Doric triglyph is not the protruding end of a ceiling beam (as it seems to pretend), nor does the metope close any intervening empty gap; no rafter carrying the roof ever beds in the overhang of the mutule, nor would a rafter be trimmed and nailed in the way which a mutule depicts; the Ionic dentils correspond to nothing behind them; and the Ionic epistyle, though functioning as a master beam for supporting the remaining entablature precisely as it appears to do, has not been assembled as its three-banded articulation pretends; and only the column shafts below and the upturned gutter along the roof above are entirely what they seem to be and in physical actuality perform the offices in which they are seen to be engaged.

The current explanation for these anomalies asserts that these structurally inactual aspects of the two Orders have resulted from transferring to stone, unmodified by any further thought, all the detail of timberwork, precisely as beam and plank were once hewn and fitted in an earlier time when such buildings were erected in wood. But this assertion will not stand even the least technically informed, intelligent scrutiny. The forms assumed by the various structural elements of the two Orders are all imitative of timber construction, truly enough; and, taken individually, they are interpretable as reproductions of wooden prototypes carved in stone. But all this is merely the idiom of their superficial appearance; and these metaphoric shapes have been assigned to them because marble or limestone, of and by itself, when fitted and assembled for walls and ceilings, to enclose and cover rooms, corridors, and porches, possesses only the squared edges and smooth faces of the rectangular blocks and beams to which it has been reduced, being otherwise wholly amorphous and devoid of any other character than an agreeable texture and hue.

In fact the current theory is in direct conflict with the evidence. If the triglyph is assumed to reproduce three upended planks held together by laying a fourth plank across their top, it must be objected that no builder would have sawed a squared tree trunk into boards only to reassemble them, when he might have used the squared beam intact. Nor would he have added a projecting strip to his epistyle beams in order to gain purchase for a horizontal cleat through which to drive a set of pegs up into the triglyph planks, when he could have nailed these fast by spiking them obliquely down to the epistyle beam before inserting the metopes. The mutules are equally illogical as literal copies of timber construction. They cannot reproduce the exposed undersides of rafters (especially as they also appear under the horizontal cornice on the façades, where no rafters run) because they are too broad and are set too close together. But if they are intended to represent some sort of transverse sheathing to weatherproof the projecting eaves from beneath, they would have had to be continuous and would never have been secured in series with an array of eighteen pegs in each. There is much else of the same sort to make it clear that no construction in wooden beams, planks, and pegs was ever put together in any sort of correspondence with the detail articulation of the Doric Order. Hence all the many efforts to explain how this Order grew out of an antecedent wooden prototype are idle, depending as they do on an erroneous initial assumption. Greek insistence on visual intelligibility and tectonic form demanded that the elements of a monumental stone structure should be appropriately distinguished so as to suggest for each a proper place and purpose within the whole, and only wooden timber-work offered a repertory of useful and intelligible patterns on which to draw for such a concept.

It is not known who first devised this ingenious synthesis of structural shapes, nor where and when his idea first found material embodiment in an actual building. But since the Doric Order was not copied from any already extant tradition and contains much which might equally logically have been formulated differently, it seems too arbitrary and too involved an invention to be anything but an individual creation. As to its universal acceptance as a prescribed architectural form throughout central and western Greek lands, and the manner of its transmission from place to place, we know nothing and can surmise little. It is, of course, possible that a single master-mason with a corps of specialized workmen travelled about, as commissions offered, like the Romanesque and Gothic master-builders of the great medieval churches – in which case the Doric Order was not only individually invented, but also personally diffused. But it is more probable that immediate and widespread approval of so extraordinarily apt a solution to the problem of endowing post-and-beam construction in stone with a coherent and striking formal pattern, sufficed to ensure its universal acceptance. On all this we have no information whatever.

Glossary

The numbers in brackets refer to the plates that
illustrate the architectural term discussed

Abacus: The flat, square slab crowning a capital [42; 47; 72].

Anta: A pilaster terminating a wall and in the Ionic Order conforming
to the base and capital of an enclosing colonnade.

Architrave: The lowest of the three main parts of an entablature
spanning the columns of an Order [42; 43; 47].

Ashlar: Squared blocks of masonry of uniform size, laid with alternating joints as in normal brickwork [53].

Capital: The crowning feature of a column. In the Doric Order, round
in cross-section and more or less parabolic in vertical profile [12; 44;
72]. In the Ionic Order four-faced and decorated with spiral volutes
[31; 43]. In the Corinthian Order, a carved construction of intricate
design [71].

Cornice: The top, projecting member of an entablature [26; 29; 41; 43].

Echinos: The Greek term for the cushion-shaped Doric capital [72].

Entasis: The very slightly convex curve profiling Doric columns of the
early classical period.

Entablature: The upper part of an Order, consisting of architrave
(*epistyle*), frieze, and cornice (*geison*) [44].

Epistyle: The Greek term for architrave.

Fascia: A plain horizontal band of rectangular section and slight projection. Specifically applied to the three superimposed bands of the
Ionic epistyle [43].

Frieze: The middle division of an entablature, between the architrave
and cornice; in the Doric Order, consisting of alternating triglyphs and
metopes; in the Ionic Order a continuous band, frequently adorned
with carved relief [31; 43].

Geison: The Greek term for cornice, normally crowned by an upturned gutter-facing termed *sima*.

Guttae: In the Doric Order, small stud-like pendants aligned (1) in a single row on the *regula* beneath the triglyphs, and (2) in three parallel rows on the soffit (under face) of the projecting cornice (*cf.* mutule) [26; 44; 47].

Metope: The approximately square slab upended between triglyphs in the frieze of the Doric Order. It is very generally decorated with relief carving [19; 41], but may be left plain.

Moulding: The contour given to projecting members. In Greek architecture used to articulate the horizontal string-courses separating the various component parts of an Order.

Mutule: The underside of a Doric cornice projecting over the triglyphs and metopes and decorated with three parallel rows of *guttae* [13; 26; 49].

Order: In Greek architecture a column, with or without a base, surmounted by a capital and supporting an entablature proportioned and decorated according to one of the three accepted modes – Doric, Ionic, Corinthian. The Doric Order was a mainland Greek invention of very early date: the Ionic Order [31; 43] originated in Asia Minor in the sixth century B.C.; the Corinthian Order was an Athenian invention of the fifth century B.C., directly derived from the Ionic, and later developed by the Romans into the prototype for the Renaissance form.

Ovolo: A moulding with a convex profile approximating the section of an ellipse [43]. In full-front view it appears egg-shaped, hence its name.

Pediment: The triangular area bounded by a horizontal cornice and the converging rooflines at front and rear of a Greek temple; very generally filled with statuary [1; 41; 49; 50]

Peristyle: A range of columns surrounding a building or flanking an open court [41; 44].

Polygonal: A style of masonry construction in which blocks of random size and outline are closely fitted together [4; 5].

Profile: Specifically the cross-section of a moulding; more generally, the contour or outline of a building or any part of it.

Regula: The short flat band below the *tenia* that carries the *guttae* on a Doric architrave [26; 44; 47].

Sima: The Greek term for the crowning element of the cornice; characterized by a convex profile [43]. Its place is sometimes taken (as on the Parthenon) by ornamental blocks covering the ends of the roof-tiles.

Stylobate: The substructure on which a colonnade stands; more specifically, the top step of such a structure, forming the stepped base of a Greek temple [45; 49].

Tenia: A continuous flat horizontal band at the top of the epistyle (architrave) of the Doric Order and surmounting the triglyphs and metopes of the frieze [26; 49].

Tholos: A circular temple or shrine.

Triglyph: A block with vertical bands and grooves, separating the metopes of a Doric frieze [13; 26; 44].

Bibliography

The following abbreviations have been employed:

A J A: *American Journal of Archaeology*

Ath. Mitt.: *Mitteilungen des deutschen archaeologischen Instituts, Athenische Abteilung*

Dinsmoor A A G: W. B. Dinsmoor, *The Architecture of Ancient Greece*, 3rd ed., London–New York, B. T. Batsford Ltd, 1950

Gruben G T T S: H. Berve and G. Gruben, *Greek Temples, Theatres, and Shrines*, New York, Harry N. Abrams (no date)

Hesperia: *Journal of the American School of Classical Studies at Athens* (The Institute for Advanced Study, Princeton, New Jersey, U.S.A.)

Jhb: *Jahrbuch des deutschen archaeologischen Instituts*

Robertson: D. S. Robertson, *A Handbook of Greek and Roman Architecture*, 2nd ed., Cambridge University Press, 1945

Tod G H I: M. N. Tod, *A Selection of Greek Historical Inscriptions to the End of the Fifth Century B.C.*, 2nd ed., Oxford, Clarendon Press, 1946

I. PARTHENON

A. PRE-PERICLEAN

1. B. H. Hill, *The Older Parthenon*, A J A xvi (1912), 535–58. An archaeological study of paramount importance, superseding earlier attempts such as, notably, W. Doerpfeld, *Der aeltere Parthenon*, Ath. Mitt. xvii (1892), 158–89.

2. W. B. Dinsmoor, *The Date of the Older Parthenon*, A J A xxxviii (1934), 408–48, with additional note, A J A xxxix (1935), 508–9, replying to

3. W. Doerpfeld, *Parthenon I, II und III*, A J A xxxix (1935), 497–507. (Our present volume continues the discussion.)

4. Dinsmoor A A G, 149f.; 170; 186 *n.*2.

The intricate problem of the purpose and relative antiquity of the underground retaining walls opposite the south flank of the temple may best be evaluated by reading

(*a*) W. Kolbe, *Die Neugestaltung der Akropolis nach den Perserkriegen*, Jhb 51 (1936), 1–64; and

(*b*) W. B. Dinsmoor, A J A xxxix (1935), 412–41.

B. PERICLEAN

Large photographic views, overall and detail, of the surviving structure are most accessibly presented in

5. L. M. Collignon, *Le Parthenon*, 2nd ed., Paris, C. Eggimans, 1926; and
6. Ch. Picard, *L'Acropole*, vol. 2 (*Le plateau supérieur*), Paris, A. Morancé, 1931.

Much more extensive detail illustrations, but of smaller size and at times of inferior quality are to be found in

7. N. Balanos, *Les monuments de l'Acropole: Relèvement et conservation*, Paris, Massin, 1938; a work of great value for its measured drawings and metrologic data.

Among the best brief descriptions with authoritative architectural comment:

8. Dinsmoor A A G, 159–69;
9. Robertson, 113–18;
10. Gruben G T T S, 373–9, with photographic illustration on plates xvi; 1–4; 8–15;
11. A. T. F. Michaelis, *Der Parthenon*, Leipzig, Breitkopf & Haertel, 1870–71, despite its age is still one of the most useful sources of information when supplemented with Jahn-Michaelis, *Arx Athenarum*, 3rd ed., Bonn, 1901.

For history of the temple since classical times and more extensive bibliography of books and articles (up to 1930):

12. W. Judeich, *Topographie von Athen*, 2nd ed., Munich, C. H. Beck, 1931, 106–12; 247–56.

13. F. C. Penrose, *An Investigation of the Principles of Athenian Architecture*, London, Macmillan, 1888, persuasively advanced the claim that in the Parthenon the deviations from a normal mean were intentional and arithmetically exact. More recently, the comprehensive measurements supplied by N. Balanos (*see* item 7) have invalidated this interpretation for many of the anomalies, though without casting doubt on the actuality of horizontal curvature in stylobate and entablature, the inclination of column axes and wall surfaces, the precision of entasis, and similar 'refinements', for which consult:

14. Dinsmoor A A G, 164–9;

15. G. P. Stevens, *Concerning the Curvature of the Steps of the Parthenon*, A J A XXXVIII (1934), 533–42;

16. G. P. Stevens, *The Curves of the North Stylobate of the Parthenon*, Hesperia XII (1943).

The modern tendency to ascribe minor deviations in the dimensions of individual blocks and the spacing of members of the Order to aesthetic choice and the masons' traditions of freehand workmanship is admirably presented in

17. J. A. Bundgaard, *Mnesicles: A Greek Architect at Work*, Gyldendal, Copenhagen, Scandinavian University Books, 1957, Ch. VI.

Since the present work does not concern itself with the Parthenon's sculptural decoration (except for the south metopes), it should be sufficient to refer to

18. A. H. Smith, *The Sculptures of the Parthenon*, London, 1910; and the pertinent sections of items 5 and 6 in the present list. Specifically for the metopes there is the recent exhaustive study by

19. F. Brommer, *Die Metopen des Parthenon*, 2 vols., Mainz, P. v. Zabern, 1967, where references to earlier studies will be found listed.

The citations of architectural mouldings refer to

20. L. T. Shoe, *Profiles of Greek Mouldings*, 2 vols., Harvard University Press, Cambridge (Mass.), 1936.

The fragmentary building accounts: *Inscriptiones Graecae* I². 339–53 (Tod G H I no. 52). Rearrangement of the fragments, interpretation, and comment are due to

21. W. B. Dinsmoor in A J A XXV (1921), 233–45.

II. PROPYLAEA

The standard publication is still

1. R. Bohn, *Die Propylaeen der Akropolis zu Athen*, Berlin, W. Spemann, 1882, with accurate plans and elevations.
2. W. B. Dinsmoor in A J A xiv (1910), 143ff., *The Gables of the Propylaea*, by rather intricate reasoning supplies some missing elements for the entablature.
3. N. Balanos, *Les monuments (see* I. 7) illustrates graphically his extensive rebuilding of the Propylaea for the Greek Ministry of Public Works during the years, 1909–17.

Good large-size photographic illustrations in

4. Ch. Picard, *L'Acropole*, vol. 1, *L'enceinte, l'entrée*, etc. (*see* I. 6).

Architectural description and discussion:

5. Gruben G T T S, 379–84, with plates 5–7;
6. Dinsmoor A A G, 198–205;
7. J. A. Bundgaard, *Mnesicles (see* I. 17), Chs. i–iii; vii–viii.

At present, the most extensive and critically best treatise on the Propylaea.

The building accounts:

8. *Inscriptiones Graecae* I². 363–7; Tod, G H I, no. 58, p. 114 f.

III. TEMPLE OF ATHENA NIKE

1. L. Ross, Ed. Schaubert, and Chr. Hansen, *Der Tempel der Nike Apteros*, Berlin, 1839, is the original publication by the group which rebuilt the temple from its dismembered blocks.

In 1936–40 during consolidation of the bastion the temple was again dismantled and re-erected, with only minor corrections:

2. A. F. Orlandos, *Nouvelles observations sur la construction du temple d'Athena Nike*, *Bulletin de Correspondance Hellénique* (1947–8), 1–38;
3. A. F. Orlandos, *Zum Tempel der Athena Nike*, Ath. Mitt. (1951), 27–48;
4. Dinsmoor A A G, 151; 185–7;

5. Gruben G T T S, 384–6;
6. I. M. Shear, *Kallikrates*, Hesperia xxxii (1963), 377–88.

For the relative dates of the Nike temple and the Propylaea:
7. H. Wrede, *Mnesikles und der Nikepyrgos*, Ath. Mitt. (1932) 74–91;
8. H. Schleif, *Nikepyrgos und Mnesikles*, Jhb (1933), 177–87;
9. J. A. Bundgaard, *Mnesicles*, 178–84.

The inscription (*Inscriptiones Graecae* I². 89):
10. W. B. Dinsmoor, A J A xxvii (1923), 318ff.;
11. Tod G HI, no. 40 (pp. 78–81);
12. B. D. Meritt, Hesperia x (1941), 307–15, (highly technical).

IV. TEMPLE OF HEPHAISTOS (Hephaisteion: 'Theseion')

Excellent summary description in
1. I. H. Hill, *The Ancient City of Athens*, London, Methuen & Co., 1953, Ch. ix, with latest restored plan in figure 12.

Architectural studies:
2. J. Stuart and N. Revett, *The Antiquities of Athens*, vol. 3, London, 1794, with excellent plans and elevations.
3. H. Koch, *Studien zum Theseustempel in Athen*, Abhandlungen der Saechsischen Akademie der Wissenschaften zu Leipzig, Phil-Hist. Klasse, vol. 47², Berlin, Akademie-Verlag, 1955. Comprehensive and full of interesting material information.
4. W. B. Dinsmoor, *Observations on the Hephaisteion*, Hesperia, Suppl. v (1941). Basic for present-day understanding of the temple.

Additional minor studies:
5. O. Broneer, *Notes on the Interior of the Hephaisteion*, Hesperia xiv (1945), 246–58.
6. B. H. Hill, *The Interior Colonnade of the Hephaisteion*, Hesperia Suppl. viii (1949), 190–208.
7. G. P. Stevens, *Some Remarks upon the Interior of the Hephaisteion*, Hesperia xix (1950), 143–64.

For the sculptural decoration:

8. Br. Sauer, *Das sogenannte Theseion und sein plastischer Schmuck*, Leipzig, Giesecke and Devrient, 1889;

9. H. Koch, *Studien zum Theseustempel (see* no. 3), Ch. VIII with figures 99–140 and plates 16–39;

10. H. A. Thompson, *The Pedimental Sculpture of the Hephaisteion*, Hesperia XVIII (1949), 230–68.

V. TEMPLE ON THE ILISSOS

1. J. Stuart and N. Revett, *The Antiquities of Athens*, new ed., London, Priestley & Weale, 1825, 29–35, plates VII–XII.

2. I. M. Shear, *Kallikrates*, Hesperia XXXII (1963), 388–99.

Brief summary description in

3. W. Judeich, *Topographie von Athen (see* I.12), 420; and

4. Dinsmoor AAG, 185.

For the frieze:

5. F. Studniczka, *Zu den Friesplatten vom ionischen Tempel am Ilissos*, Jhb XXXI (1916), 169 ff., 230 ff., and XXXVIII–IX (1923–4), 116;

6. H. Moebius, *Zu Ilissosfries und Nikebalustrade*, Ath. Mitt. LIII (1928);

7. H. Moebius, *Das Metroon in Agrai und sein Fries*, Ath. Mitt. LX–LXI (1935).

VI. TEMPLES ELSEWHERE IN ATTICA

A. TEMPLE OF ARES

Originally dedicated in the Acharnian deme, it was transported to Athens in Roman times and re-erected in the Agora, where sufficient fragments were discovered by the American excavators to enable W. B. Dinsmoor to recover the temple's architectural detail.

1. W. B. Dinsmoor, *The Temple of Ares at Athens*, Hesperia IX (1940), 1–52.

2. For the sculpture attributed to the altar consult Hesperia XX (1951), 56–9; XXI (1952), 93–5.

B. For the two other temples attributed by W. B. Dinsmoor to his unknown 'Theseion architect' consult his summary statement in

3. Dinsmoor AAG, 181f. with *n*.1.

4. W. H. P. Plommer, *Annual of the British School at Athens*, XLV (1950), 78–109 (mainly statistical).

VII. TEMPLE OF APOLLO EPIKOURIOS AT BASSAI

1. Since the first basic study by C. R. Cockerell (*The Temples of Jupiter Panhellenius at Aegina and of Apollo Epicurius near Phigaleia in Arcadia*, 1860), no definitive publication has appeared. There have been, however, a large number of partial studies, which will be found listed in Dinsmoor AAG, 364–5, with subsequent entries in AJA 72 (1968), 103, *n*.2, where F. A. Cooper's article on orientation of the adyton contains some interesting observations.

2. Dinsmoor AAG, 154–9.

3. Gruben GTTS, 351–4.

VIII. TEMPLE OF THE ATHENIANS, DELOS

1. F. Courby, *Exploration archéologique de Délos*, XII, Paris, 1931, 98ff.

2. I. M. Shear, *Kallikrates*, Hesperia XXXII (1963), 399–408.

3. Gruben GTTS, 365–6.

IX. TELESTERION AT ELEUSIS

1. F. Noack, *Eleusis: die baugeschichtliche Entwicklung des Heiligtums*, Berlin, de Gruyter, 1927. Outdated, but extremely valuable if used with discretion.

2. Gruben GTTS, 399–404.

3. Dinsmoor AAG, 113; 195–6; 233.

4. J. Travlos, Hesperia XVIII (1949), 138 ff.

5. L. Shoe, Hesperia Suppl. VIII (1949), 342 ff.

Index

Numbers in square brackets refer to plates

Erechtheion, 103: column bases, 47, 90,
[33: C, D]
Eurymedon, battle of, 69–70; booty
from, 83, 165–6

Hellenotamiai, 75, 76
Hephaisteion (Theseion), 46, 98–9, 103,
108, 111, 171, [41, 44]; anta-capital,
172–3, [75]; bibliography, 188–9;
date of construction, 46, 106; features
in common with Kimonian Parthenon, 103; Kallikrates its architect,
103; moulded wallbase, 46–7, [15]
Herodotus, quoted, 31, 44
Hill, Bert Hodge: his discovery of an
earlier Parthenon, 39, 40, 51; wrongly
identified as pre-Persian, 44, 54

IKTINOS: architect of the temple of
Apollo at Bassai, 142–6; at Olympia?,
142; at work on Periclean Parthenon,
111, 115, 128; contrasted with Kallikrates, 109; replaces Kallikrates, 46,
54, 111

Ilissos, temple on, 87–8, [30, 32];
bibliography, 189; compared with
temple of Athena Nike, 88–91, 94–6,
[32]; frieze, 34–5, 92–3; Kallikrates
its architect, 86
Ithome, 72

Kallias, peace of, 77, 85
KALLIKRATES: architect of the pre-
Periclean Parthenon, 103; builds
Acropolis wall, 83, 165–6; was
Kimon's head architect, 83; builds
Ionic temple on Ilissos, 86–8, 94;
builds Long Walls to sea, 81, 83; com-
missioned to build temple to Athena
Nike, 83–4; his artistic importance,
107–8; his career, 106; other temples,
103–6, 170–74; replaced by Iktinos, 46

KIMON: ancestry, 78; building activity,
44–6, 83, 165–6; dies in Cyprus in
450 B.C., 76; exiled, 72, 73; mentioned,
35, 37, 54; military exploits, 69–70;
political activity, 69, 70, 74, 76; pro-
Spartan, 72, 73–4; wealth and gener-
osity, 74

Marathon, battle of, 28, 29, 35
marble: Parian, for frieze of Ilissos
temple, 91; Pentelic, exclusively used
for Periclean Parthenon, 91
metopes of the Parthenon: [19, 20, 21,
22]; created for Kimonian Parthenon,
59; date relative to frieze and pediments, 55, 58; how many, 66; trimmed
down for Periclean Parthenon, 55,
64–5; where preserved, 65
Mnesikles, 136
Mouldings: 100–102, 172–4, [14, 15,
33, 75]; on anta-base from Kimonian
Parthenon, 45–6, 47, 114, [14]; on
wallbase of Hephaisteion, 46, [15]

PARTHENON

THEMISTOCLEAN: column drums in
Acropolis wall, 29–33, 47, 67, [6];
destroyed by Persians, 35; how much
built, 31–3; intended plan, 33–5;
substructure, 23–4, 26–9, 164, [3, 4];
when begun, 28–31
KIMONIAN: anta-base, 45–7, 103,
113–14, [14]; how far completed, 33,
44–6, 54–5, 66, 114, 175–6; its
architect Kallikrates, 46, 103, 106,
114; limestone bottom step, 51, 103;
location on platform, 43–4; plan,
33–5, 39–41, [10], compared with
that of Periclean Parthenon, 39–43,
[10]; re-use of columns and other
material by Iktinos, 53–5, 66, 114–15;
when begun, 37, 47, 66–7, 70, 166–7;

Some other Pelican books are described on the following pages.

The Pelican History of Art

Greek Architecture

A. W. Lawrence

'Professor Lawrence provides a survey of architectural remains in Aegean lands ranging from the end of the Stone Age to the beginning of Roman rule. This panoramic vista enables him to trace many of the characteristic features of classical Greek temple architecture back to the domestic and funeral architecture of the Bronze Age.

For the first time we have here all the relevant material of the prehistoric Aegean collected and presented as a background to the later and better known achievements of classical Greek architecture... This Pelican volume will take its place beside Dinsmoor and Robertson as an indispensable instrument for all interested in Greek architecture'—*The Times Educational Supplement*.

Style and Civilization

This series interprets the important styles in European art in the broadest context of the civilization and thought of their times. It aims, in this way, to achieve a deeper understanding of their character and motivation.

Pre-Classical *John Boardman*

The power and personality of King Minos or Agamemnon are shrouded in legend. But from surviving art and artefacts we can begin to draw pictures of the real quality of life in the Bronze Age palaces of Crete or Mycenae, or in the world of Archaic Greece after the Dark Ages. This book portrays through their art the civilizations that stand at the beginnings of the Western tradition.

Gothic *George Henderson*

Every age has held its own vision of the Gothic world – a world of barbarism, or of chivalry, or of piety. Here is an attempt to reach a deeper understanding of the Gothic style by examining its many forms in the context of contemporary religious or philosophical attitudes, and against the background of the social and political order of the Middle Ages.

Early Renaissance *Michael Levey*

Humanity and the human form dominate Early Renaissance art – from the intensely realistic figures portrayed by Van Eyck to the sophisticated beings created by Dürer or Leonardo. New techniques, discovery of visual perspective, fresh interest in the antique past, all combined to make art a fully rational activity, incorporating truths of human nature and the universe. In place of Gothic mystery came clarity – reflected in the calmly ordered space of Renaissance buildings. This book emphasizes that persistent preference for sober, logical, harmonious art – true to experience and yet optimistic – which characterizes the Early Renaissance.

and

MANNERISM
NEO-CLASSICISM

The Architect and Society

The aim of this series, is to present the great architects and architecture of the world in their social and cultural environments.

Chartres *George Henderson*

Of all the great cathedrals of Europe Chartres most vividly evokes the Age of Faith. Its sculptured portals, its stained glass, its massive walls and soaring spires, signify the deep commitment of medieval society to this kind of artistic endeavour.

The present book traces the history of the construction of the giant fabric, from its pre-Romanesque origins to the final campaign of work in the Gothic period. The architects responsible for specific parts of the structure are presented, as far as they now can be, as individual personalities expressing their own artistic temperament against an ever-changing social and intellectual background.

Inigo Jones *John Summerson*

Inigo Jones was the first English classical architect, famous in his own time (he was nine years junior to Shakespeare) and the posthumous sponsor of the Palladianism of the eighteenth century.

In this revolutionary book Sir John Summerson clears away a mass of legend in order to direct attention to the essential Inigo, basing a new assessment of his genius on the evidence of buildings and designs of undoubted authenticity. Inigo Jones emerges as a unique figure in the Europe of his time and an architect of fundamental importance.

Palladio *James S. Ackerman*

Palladio is the most imitated architect in history. His buildings have been copied all over the Western world – from Leningrad to Philadelphia – and his ideas on proportion are still current nearly four hundred years after his death. In this, the first full account of his career to be published in English, Professor James Ackerman investigates the reasons for his enormous and enduring success. He presents him in his historical setting as the contemporary of Titian, Tintoretto, and Veronese, but is constantly alert to his relevance for us today.